Strategic Value Analysis

ROGER W. MILLS

Finance, Strategy and

STRATEGIC VALUE ANALYSIS

Linking two key business issues

Design and Typeset: Mars Business Associates Ltd

Printed and bound in Great Britain by: Butler and Tanner Ltd

LIBRARY OF CONGRESS CATALOGING IN PUBLICATION DATA

Mills, Roger W.

Finance, Strategy and Strategic Value Analysis: Linking two key business issues/

Roger W. Mills

Included bibliographies and index

ISBN   1 873186 04 5

1. Finance, Strategy

I. Title

Mars Business Associates Ltd

62 Kingsmead
Lechlade
Glos. GL7 3BW

To

Stephanie, always encouraging;

Max, never out of sight for long;

and

Sable, not forgotten.

Acknowledgements

It is rare for a book to the product of a single person's endeavours. Like a stage production, many work behind the scenes to help those in the limelight deliver on the day. This book was no exception.

I should like to thank the many individuals who assisted me in the writing of the book, and specifically David Parker, James and Victoria Dimech DeBono, and Nick Weaver for their helpful suggestions. As always, any errors which remain are mine!

Preface

The business world of today is turbulent. Organisations of all types have to make choices about how to manage scarce resources in a climate so often characterised by considerable and rapid change.

In such a world sound strategic thinking, analysis and direction have been acknowledged as being particularly important, as has finance. Having identified a potential strategic option for an organisation, like a potential merger, acquisition, restructuring, buyout, alliance, partnership or joint venture, there is clearly the need to evaluate whether it will be worthwhile in financial terms. But, how should you evaluate the acceptability of a strategic option in financial terms? Is there more than one approach that can be used? Which is preferable? Why? These are some of the questions we will address in this book.

As we will demonstrate, the application of finance enables the acceptability of a particular proposed strategy to be assessed meaningfully, provided the most appropriate approach is used. This is essentially because when used properly, finance enables the creation (or destruction) of value to be measured and thus strategies may be evaluated in terms of the value they add to the organisation.

The approach developed in this book we refer to as Strategic Value Analysis. This represents an extension of the approach which has been popularised as Shareholder Value Analysis and which has gained prominence in the United States since the late 1970s. Its primary focus of attention has been upon one particular group of stakeholders, the shareholders, and it has become associated with measuring the benefit to them of potential strategic courses of action.

Strategic Value Analysis is a tool that links strategy and finance, particularly in the evaluation of potential strategic options. However, it is all too often seen as a corporate planning tool rather than an approach that can be used in managing the business. It is also seen as being somewhat restricted because of its origins which were in measuring value to shareholders of large, publicly quoted companies in developed equity markets.

The reality is that the principles that underpin Shareholder Value Analysis have been applied in some organisations more extensively than simply a corporate planning tool. Furthermore, the approach may be applied to smaller companies and in relation to less developed equity markets. For this reason we prefer to think of the approach in terms of Strategic Value Analysis. The basic principle which underpins it is discounted cash flow analysis, which makes it universally applicable beyond just the corporate environment. Even organisations without shareholders, like the National Health Service, face resource management issues for which the approach is well suited to handle.

Roger W. Mills,   March 1994.

Contents

1

Finance and Strategy

> "Must strategy and finance clash?...........Marketing and finance are
> complementary - when the analysis is right"
>
> Barwise, Marsh and Wensley [1]

Introduction

Finance and strategy need not and *must not* clash. However, as the introductory quote from *Barwise, Marsh and Wensley* emphasises, the analysis must be right. So,

- ○ What sort of analysis is important from both a strategic and financial perspective?

- ○ Why is financial analysis important in decisions associated with strategic analysis and choice?

- ○ What alternative approaches can be used for analysing strategic decisions in financial terms?

- ○ What basic principles and theories underpin contemporary business finance?

These are the key issues we will address in this chapter by way of an introduction to the rest of the book.

An understanding of the context of finance within strategic management is vital. But, as the review in this chapter will serve to show, there is more than one view about the approach to finance that should be used, and furthermore finance is not the stagnant discipline it is sometimes portrayed as being.

The strategic triangle

One well respected view about the construction of any business strategy is that three main players need to be taken into consideration - the corporation, the customer and the competition.

Figure 1.1   The strategic triangle

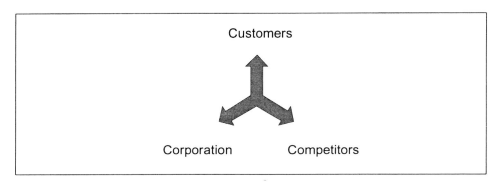

These three "C's" identified by *Kenichi Omae*[2] and *Michael Porter's* five forces[3] are supportive of a view that strategic analysis and choice is often traditionally associated with establishing superior value in the eyes of the customer or by achieving competitive advantage through outperforming competitors along dimensions like cost, technological capability, and the acquisition of raw materials.

Whilst the focus of attention in much of strategy has been towards the customer, the thinking that has dominated finance has been almost exclusively shareholder oriented. Pick up most well respected finance texts and you will find the maximisation of returns to shareholders being quoted as being the key business objective [4]. Furthermore, associated with this is the belief that success is measurable in terms of whether value will be created or destroyed.

Must strategy and finance clash? More specifically, must the customer oriented marketing view and the shareholder oriented financial view necessarily conflict with one another? This was a question posed by *Barwise, Marsh and Wensley* in the *Harvard Business Review* [5]. Not so they argued provided the analysis is right. What they identified as being required is an interactive process that relates the product-market specifics to wider financial implications. In fact, as we will demonstrate in this book, Strategic Value Analysis, or SVA, can be seen as providing this interactive process.

Furthermore, the SVA approach is adaptable to changes within both disciplines. For example, in the last fifteen or so years there has been a discernible move within strategy towards a focus of attention upon what it is that makes firms different. Much evidence suggests that the performance achieved by an organisation depends more upon its relative performance within an industry rather than the industry it is in. For example, *Richard Rumelt* analysed the returns of a large sample of American firms by reference to their profitability in different industries [6]. *Rumelt's* findings are summarised in *Table 1.1*:

Table 1.1   Contributions to variance of profits across business units

	%
Corporate ownership	0.8
Industry effects	8.3
Cyclical effects	7.8
Business unit specific effects	46.4
Unexplained factors	36.7

Source: R. P. Rumelt, "How much does industry matter?",   Strategic Management Journal, March 1991.

By far the largest contributor to explaining differences in profits is business unit-specific effects. In other words, there are no systematically successful firms or industries, but there are systematically successful business units. These are the businesses that enjoy competitive advantages and outperform their competitors year by year.

Such observations stimulated research by *John Kay* to identify what are the core capabilities that can give businesses an edge [6]. He moved away from a profit oriented focus which presents many difficulties we will review in a later chapter, and based upon his analysis of added value has identified four types of distinctive capability:

1. reputation
2. architecture
3. innovation
4. strategic assets

For example, he argues that reputation enables a company to charge higher prices, or gain larger market share at a competitive price, for a functionally equivalent product. Reputation he cites as being important to *Lloyds Bank* (a company we will discuss later in *Chapter 9)* and *Sainsbury's*, the food retailing supermarket chain.

Architecture is viewed in terms of a unique structure of relationships in or around the company, that is between the company and its suppliers. *Sainsbury's* is identified by *Kay* as enjoying both types of architecture, but so are other successful companies like *Marks and Spencer* and *Benetton*.

Innovation is seen as being a very strong source of competitive advantage, but one which is difficult to sustain because of the potential for replication. Patent protection can play an important part in reaping the benefits from innovation, but may be difficult to achieve in practice. One noteworthy exploiter of this approach has been the pharmaceuticals industry and indeed *Glaxo* is a good example of a company that has a track record of benefiting as regards the value added generated.

The last of these distinctive capabilities, the ownership of strategic assets, differs from the others because they are the product of the market or regulatory environment rather than of a company's distinctive achievement.

These four distinctive capabilities are important and we will review them more fully in a later chapter, where we will illustrate how an understanding of them can be seen as complementing the SVA framework, and vice versa. They will also be viewed alongside the related core competences approach associated with *Prahalad and Hamel* [8]. This focuses upon the development of a strategic architecture to identify and commit the technical and production linkages across business units so as to build upon distinct skills and capabilities that cannot be matched or easily replicated by other organisations.

As regards SVA, you may have encountered it under the heading of Shareholder Value Analysis, a term developed in the United States and brought to prominence by *Alfred Rappaport* [9]. Much of what we will provide as a financial framework under the banner of Strategic Value Analysis is attributable to the work of *Rappaport* and others. However, we have deliberately chosen to broaden the term because we believe it implies a very narrow field of application towards large profit oriented corporations. Contrary to this view we believe that the principles are applicable to organisations of all types.

Time and value

It is important to introduce time at this point. A major criticism levelled against Britain and America in recent years has been short-termism, often viewed in terms of the poor relative competitive edge by these two countries as being attributable to their failure to emphasise long-term investment, this in turn being the fault of their myopic financial markets.

A noteworthy review of short-termism has been undertaken by *Paul Marsh* who finds little to support the view that financial markets play any significant part in promoting a short-termist perspective [10]. However, he did find managerial short-termism to represent a real problem, an issue well summarised in his concluding note:

> *"The way ahead for both City and industry is for UK managers*
>
> *to get on with managing as if tomorrow mattered."*

Many businesses in Britain do appear to adopt a very short-termist perspective, that is managing for today rather than tomorrow and beyond. However, having faced arguably the worst recession since the 1930s who can blame British business people for tending to adopt such a perspective and, as we will illustrate, the world of accounting and finance has done little to avert such thinking.

SVA represents an important alternative to taking a short-termist perspective which can be applied to take consideration of the short-term financial needs of an organisation as well as its longer term objectives. Whilst it will initially be developed with reference to the corporate environment it can be applied in principle in any sector of the economy to help managers in making the best use of the resources at their disposal.

The importance of finance

We live in an increasingly turbulent society characterised by very rapid change. One feature of this society is that organisations of all types have to make strategic choices which usually have to be evaluated in financial terms.

What are such strategic choices? Should we:

○ Enter a new line of business?

○ Acquire a new business?

○ Divest non-core activities?

○ Form a strategic alliance? and so on.

Imagine not evaluating such choices in financial terms. It is almost unthinkable. For example, imagine *ICI's* demerger plan not being evaluated in financial terms, or for that matter the decision by *BMW* to buy *Rover.* In such cases, there is a need for financial analysis to guide the decisions that management will often have to make.

Strategic choices often have to be made following, or in anticipation of, some change in the business environment in which the enterprise exists. Whilst some choices may be voluntary others are imposed by the course of action taken by others and the potential course(s) of action are consequently far more limited. To return to an earlier example, *BMW*, decision to buy the 80% stake in *Rover Cars* held by *British Aerospace* was a voluntary decision, but it had a "knock-on" effect upon *Honda* which held the remaining 20%. As a consequence of the sale, *Honda* felt forced to re-evaluate its European strategy and, accordingly, its strategic options.

Outside the private sector organisations of all types also have to respond to strategic issues. A good example of this can be seen in National Health Service in the UK where reform has meant a response of quite a different order to that of the past. In this and other areas of what was previously referred to as the Public Sector in the UK, many initiatives and drives towards more commercial practices have had a significant impact upon the strategic direction such organisations take.

One key point about strategic choice is that while a case may be made for possible courses of action in conceptual terms, there is always the need to be able to express the outcome in financial terms All business decisions have financial consequences and any alternatives need be compared in order to select what is hoped will represent the most desirable course of action. Because of its concern with measurement and the evaluation of business activity, finance has a vital role to play. For example, it is in financial terms that enterprises express many targets - in terms of growth rates and target future earnings - which they aim to achieve. Future plans are also typically quantified using financial measures to see whether long-term objectives will be or, indeed, can be achieved.

For companies whose shares are traded in the stock market, financial objectives and measures have become pre-eminent. The reason for this is that they have to attract capital in the market place and it is there - in the capital markets (the stock markets) - that the available capital will be allocated to the companies offering the highest returns. Nonetheless, organisations in the not-for-profit sector - for example, in public education, public health, public transport and in charitable organisations - are also competing for economic resources. They have to set out plans which will attract public funds by presenting a strong case for funds.

For the moment let us focus upon for profit organisations, which exist to provide products or services to customers in a market place at home or abroad for a profit. In such businesses it is hoped, or rather, it is planned, that a profit is made through such enterprise and that profit offers a return to the providers of finance, it is their incentive to invest. In such a commercial world, a business will seek to attract funds either from shareholders or from lenders. Each of these providers of finance expects to receive a return on the investment made and they are giving up some cash now for a cash return later. The manner in which they receive this cash return differs somewhat depending on whether the investor is a shareholder or a lender.

Shareholders have their proportionate ownership of the company divided into equal parcels - *stocks or shares*. Each share carries with it an equal (or equitable) share of the business. Thus, such capital has become known as *equity*. Lenders, on the other hand, do not own a share of the business, although they have prior rights to the company's assets in the event of the company winding up. As the loans have to be repaid in due course, such borrowing by a company is often known as *debt*. We shall be using the terms *debt* and *equity* through this book.

Figure 1.2   Main providers of finance - the two extremes

Shareholders receive their return by way of an annual cash payment known as a dividend. The dividend is usually a relatively small percentage of the market value of the underlying shares.

Shareholders also expect that the value of their shares will grow. This growth is achieved because companies do not pay out all profits made by way of dividends. Some profit will be retained and reinvested in the business, thus growing the value of the company for the shareholders who own it. This part of the "return" of the shareholders is somewhat risky because no-one can be sure of the rate of growth, if any, that the invested funds will achieve. For this reason, a shareholder expects a higher total return (dividend plus share growth) than does a lender to a company.

The lender does not normally take such risks. The lender usually expects to receive a rate of interest annually on the capital invested and the promise of the repayment of the capital invested at some future date. However, there are exceptions, such as where businesses fail, which may result in the complete loss of funds invested.

In not-for-profit organisations where activities are controlled by central and local government, or in charities, the intended aim will not normally be to make a profit as a return to providers of finance. Such organisations will aim to provide goods and/or services within the constraints imposed by cash available from funds or grants provided by government, or from charitable donations. They may also aim to make a "surplus" or seek capital grants. For example, a children's home charity may use any surplus income in excess of running costs to build (or buy) a new home so that more children can be supported.

Objectives and financial targets

Organisations often focus upon a few critical objectives. For example, in the annual report and accounts produced since 1989 of the international banking group, *Standard Chartered plc*, reference has been made to the pursuit of the following strategic objectives [12]:

- ○ to focus on our strengths

- ○ to improve our underlying profitability

- ○ to manage our capital base

- ○ to tackle our problem country debt

- ○ to develop our performance-based culture

The pursuit of such objectives is bound to have financial implications. Focusing upon strengths may necessitate the disposal of peripheral businesses and the loss of some revenues that contribute to profit but a gain in cash from disposal receipts. Similarly, the development of a performance-based culture may require an investment in people and, therefore, having to incur a short-term loss of earnings because of the cost of training in order to gain in the longer term.

Objectives are typically used to set financial targets so that managers who wish to undertake projects within an enterprise have some guidance as to the result that needs to be forecast (and achieved!) from their proposals. In a commercial enterprise this means that the assessment of how well the cash will be spent would conventionally be made by comparing the budgeted performance from the proposed activities, with a return required by the providers of finance. So if a return of 15% is the objective, only projects which are expected to achieve this return will be accepted. In principle, the concept of return is quite obvious - What return will be achieved for a certain amount of investment, that is what future benefits will result from expenditure now?

From management's point of view it will be quite clear what a lender expects to receive. A lender will be offered a certain rate of annual interest for a loan of capital today. The offer to shareholders is rather more complicated. The shareholder will expect to be offered some annual cash return by way of a dividend with the expectation (or hope?) that the shares owned will grow in value. This growth in share value should result because not all of the company's profits are distributed. Some earnings are retained and they are re-invested in the business in new projects and provided those projects perform well the share price will grow.

Companies will also typically have targets which are subsidiary, but often linked, to the overall aim of investing at the best return on investment/capital employed used in its generation. A good example of such ratios can be seen with reference to the *General Electric Company (GEC) plc*, a major electronics group in the UK. Since 1968, senior *GEC* management has been reported as using ratios from amongst the following seven key criteria to monitor the performance of the *GEC* divisions:

1. Profit on capital employed

2. Profit on sales

3. Sales as a multiple of capital employed

4. Sales as a multiple of fixed assets

5. Sales as a multiple of stocks

6. Sales per employee

7. Profits per employee

These seven can be related to one another within a framework such that the effects of improving one of them can be traced through and measured for the business as a whole.

Ratios can be thought of acting as prompts in the overall planning objective of achieving the best use of the cash available for investment. A key reason for wanting to make the best use of capital resources is that a company with historically good returns will be able to attract the capital required for new projects in a competitive capital market, or put another way, if it fails to achieve good returns its share price will fall potentially making it a very attractive take-over proposition. As a consequence, one financial ratio, Return (Profit) On Capital Employed, believed to be indicative of financial performance has been pre-eminent in accounting and finance.

Return On Capital Employed (ROCE)

Return On Capital Employed (ROCE), may be calculated in a number of ways and in fact how it will be used will depend upon what one is trying to measure. Consider a company with:

○ £100m total assets after deducting current liabilities

○ which is financed by £30m loan capital and £70m equity

○ has annual profits (ignoring taxation) of £25m before interest charges

○ and interest on loan capital amounts to 10% per annum.

The Return On Capital Employed may be measured in a number of ways. Two popular alternatives are referred to as the Return On Net Assets (RONA) and the Return On Equity (ROE). There is no clear view about which of the two ratios is best described as the Return On Capital Employed (ROCE). Whereas RONA indicates the overall return on capital no matter what was the long-term source of that capital, ROE measures just the return on the funds provided by shareholders, ignoring the interest paid to the lenders of the loan capital.

Using the above data the result of calculating these two ratios would be:

$$\text{Return On Net Assets} = \frac{£25m}{£100m} \times 100$$

$$= 25\%$$

$$\text{Return On Equity} = \frac{£25m - £3m \text{ (interest)}}{£100m - £30m \text{ (debt)}} \times 100$$

$$= 31\%$$

This example serves to illustrate one important shortcoming of many conventionally used financial measures - *there appears to be a considerable degree of choice.* This is made even more complex when one considers that for companies with publicly traded shares, market value calculations can also be undertaken for the Return On Equity! For example, if the company above had 100m ordinary shares, each with a market value of 88p then the ROE using market values would be:

$$\text{Return On Equity} = \frac{£25m - £3m \text{ (interest)}}{100m \times 88p} \times 100$$

$$= 25\%$$

To be fair, frameworks have been developed to show how ratios like return on net assets and return on equity are positioned within a hierarchy of ratios like that illustrated earlier for *GEC*, but this still does not overcome other shortcomings that we will review.

Profit or cash measures of return?

There are many shortcomings of profit oriented measures of return that we will consider at length in *Chapter 3*. Fortunately, as we will demonstrate, cash flow analysis can be used to overcome these difficulties and has a well established pedigree in evaluating the future benefits of capital projects in present day terms. In fact, many strategic decisions can be seen as being analogous to capital projects because they involve taking a view that spans many years.

Some types of capital projects actually have strategic implications. An obvious example of this is the channel tunnel, but there are many others. For example, consider a mining organisation's decision to invest in a mine or the decision by an oil company like *BP* or *Shell* to invest in an oilfield. These are examples of strategic investments with very obvious long term implications. In other business environments time horizons are often viewed as being much shorter, although for strategic purposes this may not be so. It may simply be the case that to plan beyond say five years is difficult and there may be little faith in resulting numbers. However, this is not to say that strategic plans should not *in principle* be much longer.

Exactly how finance can help to ensure that any value beyond a period within which forecasts can be comfortably made we reserve for later. For now let us acknowledge that the evaluation of any strategic option can be viewed as being much the same as the evaluation of any decision with long-term implications, for which there is a well developed financial framework built around discounted cash flow analysis. As we will show, this can be applied within a strategic context and overcomes a significant shortcoming of many conventional profit-oriented approaches for evaluating strategic options which are reliant upon accounting information and are particularly oriented towards a profit making environment.

A clear advantage with cash flow analysis which should not be overlooked is that it is applicable to organisations of all types including profit and non profit organisations, irrespective of whether they are private or public. For example, it can be used to meet the challenge of evaluating a strategic option relating to a part of a business, or to an organisation like a National Health Service trust, for which there is no company quoted share price. As is clear, for evaluating such strategic options we need a means of evaluating strategic plans which does not depend on stock market prices.

The key challenge as regards cash flow analysis is actually the generation of robust forecasts of future cash flows over a relevant time period. As you will see in a later chapter, such cash flows can be derived by looking at what it is that drives them. By applying this approach, cash inflows and outflows can be forecast for future time periods. Equally, difficult practical issues like risk, uncertainty, inflation and taxation that often have very important implications for a decision can also be readily incorporated.

Whilst we have flagged the need for a framework relevant to the needs of all types of organisation, we do have to bear in mind that, as with many things in business life, there are certain historical conventions and traditions that may well be applied in analysing and evaluating opportunities. These conventions and traditions have their origins in the world of accounting and you will often find that a good deal of accounting information is used for evaluating strategic options. However, by the time you have finished this book you should be able to recognise how to deal with such information appropriately.

Key concepts of finance

We have highlighted the importance of cash flow analysis, but there is a problem - how can you add the cash flows from successive years when they are not comparable? For example, if you were offered £100,000 now or in one year, you would not be indifferent between the two choices. Leaving aside any loss in purchasing power as a result of inflation, you could clearly invest £100,000 today to produce more than £100,000 in a year. Quite how much more would depend upon the rate of return you require and that which is available. This principle, which we develop more fully later in *Chapter 4*, underpins discounted cash flow analysis, a concept well grounded within financial theory. For many years the maximisation of shareholders' wealth measured using the discounted cash flow technique, net present value or present value rule, has been accepted. As the *Table 1.2* illustrates the present value rule is far from new, but has gained increasing acceptance in recent years.

Table 1.2   *Present Value Rule*

○   Fisher-Hirshleifer Model - *Fisher* (1930) and *Hirshleifer* (1958) [11]
○   The rule proved why in a world of certainty accepting all projects with a positive NPV maximises the wealth of shareholders.

If you pick up many texts on finance you may well gain the impression that the whole subject area is akin to a natural science. It is true that the subject area may be approached by many scientifically, but the testing process is far more exacting than other subjects because of the number and complexity of variables involved. One analogy sometimes made is between the weather and finance, but there is one vital difference. The causes of the weather are the same now as they were yesterday and even hundreds of years ago: humidity, pressure differentials, sea-surface temperatures, and so on. Whilst depressions cause rain and are considered as having always done so, financial markets change all the time. As regards finance, the world is in a state of perpetual change. For example, oil prices were a powerful influence on the bond market during the Gulf War, but are not always.

You might be surprised to find how much change there can be in finance, a point we will reinforce with reference to three key concepts that underpin numerous contemporary financial applications - the efficient market hypothesis, portfolio theory, and the Capital Asset Pricing Model.

In what follows we will illustrate the dynamic nature of the subject with reference to these three concepts. We have also summarised the chronology of financial developments by way of a number of tabulated checklists.

The first of these concepts, the efficient market hypothesis gave quite a clear message - there is no way to beat the market. Anyone who was lucky enough to do so would not be able to sustain the advantage over the long term because information flows swiftly into the market where it reaches investors who react immediately. Their decisions to buy or sell will drive prices quickly to a point where shares are fully valued and only unforeseen events can affect those prices. Such unforeseen events can affect share prices both positively and negatively which means that there are no clear trends in the movement of shares.

Table 1.3   Efficient Markets Hypothesis

○ Attributable to *Eugene Fama*,1965 [13]
○ The main implication of market efficiency is that, as far as we can tell, share prices can be trusted - given the existing stock of publicly available information shares will neither be over - nor under - valued.
○ There is no way to beat the market other than by getting information faster.
○ Current prices reflect all information about a security.
○ Only unpredictable news can cause a change in prices; old news has already been discounted.
○ Because unpredictable news is unpredictable, price changes are unpredictable and follow a "random walk".

Key within the efficient markets hypothesis were two important ideas, the first being that investors are rational, and second, that rational investors trade only on new information, not on intuition. Such a belief that investors are rational gave rise to a pillar of modern finance to which we will make extensive reference, the Capital Asset Pricing Model, otherwise known as CAPM. This presumes that rational investors will seek a premium from risky investments and sets out to define the risk premium of a share in relation to the market. The model attempts both to predict market behaviour and to serve as a tool to help corporate managers invest in those projects that the market will value positively.

CAPM was developed from portfolio theory which quite simply suggests that an investor who diversifies will do better than one who does not. This simple observation helped to stimulate the development of a whole new wave of investment products - including the investment index funds - which seen in conjunction with the efficient market hypothesis reinforced the message to investors that there was *no way to beat the market.* Quite simply, if it is not possible to beat the market, then a sensible investor will simply hold the market in the form of a basket of shares that in some way represents all the markets upside potential while trying to diversify all the downside risks.

Table 1.4   Portfolio Theory

> ○ Attributable to *Markowitz* [14].
>
> ○ 2 important points:
>
> 1. Risk in investment appraisal is defined by the amount of variation of returns over time.
>
> 2. Overall risk may be reduced (relative to return) if assets are combined into portfolios.

From such portfolio theory it became a logical step to develop a model to permit judging the risk of any one share in relation to the market as a whole. This is achieved by a measure of the volatility of one share in relation to the market as a whole, known as a beta.

Just how is this beta determined? Few business opportunities have the same degree of risk attached to them and it should not come as any surprise that the providers of finance will expect to be compensated for greater risk by demanding a greater return. The real challenge is to get a handle upon such risk. This can be achieved by using CAPM referred to earlier. More specifically, this is a statistical model developed in the mid-1960's, which is based upon the observation that some shares are more volatile than others. This means that when stock markets rise these shares rise faster and higher than the markets, and when the stock markets fall they fall faster and further.

If markets use information efficiently such that share prices are adjusted quickly and continue to reflect new information about a company's risks and prospects, the fact that some shares are riskier than the average it is considered should reflect something about the riskiness of their underlying business. Armed with this it is possible to measure the sensitivity of a share's price to market movements by calculating its beta. The most common method of estimating beta is using regression techniques based upon historical share price movements. The historical estimation period generally accepted is five years, using monthly returns. This is the method used by the major beta provider in the UK, the *London Business School's Risk Measurement Service* [15].

Table 1.5   Capital Asset Pricing Model (CAPM)

> ○ Attributable to *Sharpe*,1964 [16].
>
> ○ The return on any risky asset is the risk free interest rate plus a risk premium which is a multiple of the beta and the premium on the market as a whole.
>
> ○ Security prices include discounts for certain sorts of risks, which alone explain consistently higher returns by some investors.
>
> ○ The more volatile a portfolio of securities, the lower its price for a given return. Therefore, the only way to get higher returns on a portfolio in the long run is to accept higher risks.

The market as a whole has a beta of one. Any share moving in line with the market would also have a beta of one. A share twice as volatile as the market (that is when the market climbs 10% it climbs 20%) would have a beta of two; one that is half as volatile would have a beta of one-half.

Concerns about measuring risk using a beta have been raised by a number of academics resulting in the development of a multi-factor model known as Arbitrage Pricing Theory (APT) that is claimed to be far more effective in predicting the markets.

Table 1.6   Arbitrage Pricing Theory (APT)

○ Attributable to *Ross*, 1976 [17].
○ The principle which underpins APT is that two assets that have identical risk characteristics must offer the same return or an arbitrage opportunity will exist.
○ APT attempts to measure the various dimensions of market related risk in terms of several underlying economic factors, such as inflation, monthly production and interest rates, which systematically affect the price of all shares.
○ In a nutshell, regression techniques are used to estimate the contribution made by each APT factor to overall risk.

However, even this approach has been questioned and a number of problems have been identified. These are summarised in *Table 1.7*:

Table 1.7   Problems with APT

○ The approach is more complex than CAPM and not without some difficulties in terms of its application.
○ This has been recognised in terms of its application in the US where, for example, the monthly production figures published by the government are only estimates of true US industrial production.
○ This means that they are "noisy" (contain random errors) and inaccurate (contain biases introduced by the data-gathering procedure and the government smoothing or adjustment process).
○ Error thus arises because high quality data in the form of share prices is regressed against lower quality data.
○ Means have been devised to overcome such problems and to operationalise the approach and a significant improvement in the explanatory power of APT over CAPM has been demonstrated.

What really brought the whole issue to a head was that *Eugene Fama*, whose efficient market work underpinned much of what is considered to be "modern finance", concluded that beta was the wrong measure of risk.

Fama, in conjunction with his colleague *Kenneth French*, concluded that the Capital Asset Pricing Model does not describe the last 50 years of average share returns [18]. Their observations are summarised in *Table 1.8*:

Table 1.8   Beta as a measure of risk

○ CAPM does not explain why returns on shares differ, quite simply beta is not a good guide.
○ All financial shares traded on NYSE, AMEX and NASDAQ between 1963 and 1990 were analysed and were grouped into portfolios.
○ When grouped on the basis of size (market capitalisation), CAPM provided an explanation of differences in returns, but each portfolio contained a wide range of betas.
○ Shares were also grouped by firm size and the ratio of book value to market value and provided a better explanation of differences in returns than betas.
○ Conclusion - size and market to book ratios are best indicators of likely returns.

In spite of the work by *Fama and French*, others reckon the results can be explained without discarding beta. How? Well, the view of such individuals is that:

1. Investors may irrationally favour big firms.

2. They may lack the cash to buy enough shares to spread risk completely, so that risk and return are not perfectly matched in the market.   *unreliable information*

3. There may be "noise" in the CAPM beta.

However, the direct implications of the work by *Fama and French* are that if beta is not the appropriate predictor of risk then perhaps risk is not related to return in the way financial theorists have predicted for the past two decades. This would mean that either the markets are not efficient in the way that we have understood them to be, or that the Capital Asset Pricing Model is the wrong model, or both.

The current situation is that these controversial empirical findings, when combined with a good deal of criticism of the Capital Asset Pricing Model, leave financial theory in turmoil. However, there is a view that it may be possible to understand what is happening using chaos theory. Like earlier market theorists, the chaos school begins with science, drawing upon "cutting-edge" work in physics, maths and computing. Those involved are using new mathematical techniques to view the markets as complex and evolving systems. At the heart of their search is a belief that you can unlock the secrets of any situation if you can get the right perspective.

An analogy with a simple traffic accident can be used to illustrate the chaos perspective. If you get in your car and follow your normal route to work but then turn a corner and collide with another car, the accident seems random to you. However, if you are watching the two cars from a helicopter overhead, the collision may well seem to be inevitable. The chaos school with its focus of attention upon physics and mathematics believe that properly observed, apparently random events like the movement of stock prices will show themselves to be, if not predictable, then at least decipherable.

Whilst the chaos school seems rather far afield from traditional finance, it is attracting much attention, but unfortunately those involved have tended to develop multidimensional market models which only a privileged few can understand. The plain fact of the matter is that because of their complexity, the models are simply useless to senior management. For this reason we are probably unlikely to see the death of the Capital Asset Pricing Model, or the efficient markets hypothesis. Quite simply, no one has come up with a workable alternative. Instead of throwing out the old financial models in favour of new ones, senior managers are likely to find it more helpful to use the new concepts to understand the assumptions and limitations that are built into the models they have been using all along. However, the chaos theorists may well be able to help managers think about investments in new ways and to question some of the assumptions of the old ones.

Some believe that the Capital Asset Pricing Model and Arbitrage Pricing Theory can still be applied. For example, *Roll and Ross* [19] argue on the basis of their work that one cannot conclude that Capital Asset Pricing Theory is dead. In terms of our concern with value, the implications are that whilst the techniques associated with the theory as regards CAPM and APT may be limited, they can be made more effective operationally by using a robust peer group or industry average return as a measure of market related risk. This will also help overcome some of the acknowledged problems of the two approaches, which may be summarised as:

○ Both assume that the past is a good representation of the future, a view that is clearly flawed for businesses undergoing or which have undergone a period of substantial structural change.

○ Since beta is measured by regressing returns over a long period of time (usually 5 years), the effect of the change on the company's beta will be slow to appear. Thus, the historical beta of a company that has recently changed its exposure to risk may not be a good estimate of its future beta.

○ Last, neither approach can be used directly for firms, divisions or other business entities that do not have publicly traded shares.

Concluding remarks

In drawing together two disciplines like strategy and finance there is much groundwork to cover in each. The purpose of this chapter has been to provide such groundwork and also the context for the following chapters which consider:

Chapter 2   An overview of Strategic Value Analysis practices and an introduction to Meunier plc, the example company.

3   The shortcomings of accounting and conventional financial analysis practices and the benefit of cash flow for Strategic Value Analysis.

4   A review of the tools and techniques associated with DCF analysis for evaluating strategic investment opportunities.

5 & 6   The development of the Strategic Value Analysis approach from generating cash flows based on business judgement building upon Meunier plc, the example company introduced in *Chapter 2*.

7   The issues associated with estimating the cost of capital, an essential but potentially complex component of strategic value.

8   How to apply Strategic Value Analysis, for example in evaluating a potential acquisition.

9   The issues associated with applying Strategic Value Analysis as a tool for managing a business.

These eight chapters can be read from two through to nine. However, you might wish to use the chapter preview we have provided above to help you find you way through in a manner which best suits you.

References

1. Barwise P., Marsh P. R., and Wensley R., "Must Strategy and Finance Clash?", Harvard Business Review, September - October, 1989, p 85.

2. Omae K., The Mind of the Strategist: Business Planning for Competitive Advantage, McGraw-Hill, 1982.

3. Porter M. E., Competitive Strategy: Techniques for Analysing Industries and Competitors, The Free Press, 1980.

4. Brigham E., Fundamentals of Financial Management, The Dryden Press, 1992.

5. Barwise P., Marsh P. R., and Wensley R., "Must Strategy and Finance Clash?", Harvard Business Review, September - October, 1989, pp. 85-90.

6. Rumelt R. P., "How much does industry matter?", Strategic Management Journal, Vol., No. 3, March 1991, pp.167-186.

7. Kay J., Foundations of Corporate Success: How business strategies add value, Oxford University Press, 1993.

8. Prahalad C. K. and Hamel G., "The core competence of the corporation", Harvard Business Review, Vol. 68(3), May-June, 1990, pp. 79-93.

9. Rappaport A., Creating Shareholder Value: The New Standard For Business Performance, The Free Press, 1986.

10. Marsh P., Short-termism on Trial, Institutional Fund Managers' Association, 1990.

11. Standard Chartered plc, Report and Accounts, 1989-1992.

12. Fisher I., "Theory of Interest" (1930), Macmillan, New York and Hirshleifer J., "On the Theory of Optimal Investment Decisions", Journal of Political Economy, 1958, pp. 329-372.

13. Fama E. F., "The Behaviour of Stock Market Prices", Journal of Business, January, 1965, pp. 34-105.

14. Markowitz H., Portfolio Selection, (1959) Yale University Press, New Haven.

15. London Business School Risk Measurement Service, Sussex Place, Regent's Park, London, NW1 4SA.

16. Sharpe W. F., "Capital Asset Prices: A Theory of Market Equilibrium Under Conditions of Risk", Journal of Finance, Sept. 1964, pp. 425-442.

17. Ross S. A., "The Arbitrage Theory of Capital Pricing", Journal of Economic Theory, December, 1976, pp. 343-362.

18. Fama E. F. and French K. R., "The Cross-Section of Expected Stock Returns" ,University of Chicago Centre for Research in Security Prices, 1991, and Fama E. F. and French K. R., "The Cross-Section of Expected Stock Returns", The Journal of Finance, June 1992, pp. 427-465.

19. Roll R. and Ross S. A., "On the Cross-Sectional Relation Between Expected Returns and Betas", Working Paper #21, Yale School of Management, 1992.

2

Ratios and Strategic Financial Analysis

> *"The City has gone through a period of infatuation*
> *with earnings per share and the resultant P/E ratio ...."*
>
> *Richard Hannah, UBS Phillips & Drew*

Introduction

What are the main ratios that can be used for strategic financial analysis? How do organisations use these ratios? How can information about peer group organisations be used to assist strategic financial analysis? These are the main questions we will answer in this chapter.

The focus of attention will be upon ratio analysis. We commence with a review of its general application by way of a lead into its use for purposes of strategic financial analysis. Particular attention is then paid to the use of peer group analysis both for competitive benchmarking and subsequently for estimating business value using key ratios, like the price earnings (PE) and market to book (MB) ratios. In fact, the link we develop between such ratios and business value can help to place the quote at the beginning of this chapter in context.

Review of ratio analysis

There are many profit-related performance measures in the form of financial ratios that can be and are used in managing a business. As we will illustrate, these can be readily calculated from financial statements and supporting accounting data. In *Chapter 1* we provided an illustration of some with reference to the *General Electric Company (GEC) plc*, a major electronics group in the UK. Since 1968, senior *GEC* management has been reported as using ratios from amongst the following seven key criteria to monitor the performance of the *GEC* divisions

1. Profit on capital employed

2. Profit on sales

3. Sales as a multiple of capital employed

4. Sales as a multiple of fixed assets

5. Sales as a multiple of stocks

6. Sales per employee

7. Profits per employee

These seven can be related to one another within a framework such that the effects of improving one of them can be traced through and measured for the business as a whole.   Let us consider how the first three of these are related.

The first of these ratios, profit on capital employed we encountered in *Chapter 1* as Return On Capital Employed, or ROCE. In that chapter we illustrated that there is more than just one interpretation of ROCE. However, for now, let us focus our attention specifically upon one definition, Return On Net Assets, or RONA for short. It seeks to answer the question, what return (profit) is generated from the net assets (fixed assets plus current assets less current liabilities) employed in its generation. It can be subdivided into two inter-related component ratios:

- ○   Return on sales
- ○   Sales generation

The relationship between these three and others may be expressed in the form of a so-called "pyramid" of ratios. Part of this pyramid is illustrated in *Figure 2.1*. The three RONA related ratios are shown in bold, followed by the basis for their calculation, and the name given to these three ratios in the GEC hierarchy is provided in parentheses:

Figure 2.1   *The RONA related ratios*

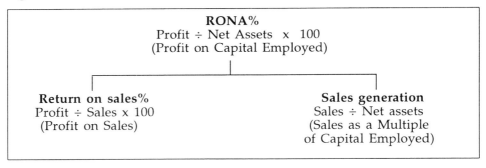

Very simply, the relationship between these three is:

$$\frac{Profit \times 100}{Net\ assets} = \frac{Profit \times 100}{Sales} \times \frac{Sales}{Net\ assets}$$

The profit generated on net assets can be further analysed in terms of the profit margin generated on sales and the net assets employed in generating those sales.

This type of analytical approach is common to accounting and finance texts and you may well be asking why it is important here. Well, the answer is that the comparison of performance against that of competitors is vital in strategic financial analysis. This type of approach can be extremely useful as a starting point.

To put these three ratios in context let us consider the following example which uses data adapted from the accounts of *Meunier plc*. *Meunier* is a publishing company that operates a number of bookstores and a number of other businesses in the UK. Its published accounts are provided in the Appendix at the end of this chapter, and include:

- ○ Consolidated profit and loss account
- ○ Consolidated balance sheet
- ○ Relevant notes to the accounts.

Using this information about *Meunier* we have calculated the RONA%, return on sales, and sales generation ratios in *Table 2.1*.

Table 2.1   Meuniers RONA related ratios

Ratios	How to calculate ratios	1993	1992	1991
1. RONA%	c ÷ e x 100 - %	12.6%	15.8%	23.1%
2. Return on sales%	c ÷ d x 100 - %	5.7%	7.4%	10.8%
3. Sales generation	d ÷ e - x *(times)*	2.2x	2.1x	2.1x
	Where to look	1993 £m	1992 £m	1991 £m
a. Profit before tax	Profit and loss account	8.7	9.4	16.3
b. Interest payable	Note 1 to accounts	3.4	5.3	3.9
c. Profit before interest and tax	a + b	12.1	14.7	20.2
d. Sales	Profit and loss account (turnover)	210.6	199.6	187.4
e. Net assets	Balance sheet (total assets less current liabilities)	96.0	93.0	87.4

(handwritten annotation above "2. Return on sales%": Sales margin)

The RONA% for *Meunier* for 1993 was 12.6%, but is this good or bad? In truth without something against which to compare this figure we have nothing particularly useful. How could it be made more meaningful? Well by having something against which to evaluate it, which could be in the form of:

- ○ An historical trend
- ○ A comparison with competitors in the same sector
- ○ A comparison with averages for the industry

For *Meunier plc*, we do have the historical data for three years against which to measure the company's performance.   So, with this in mind, let us consider the historical trend for RONA, and then what has happened to return on sales and sales generation.

RONA has decreased from 23.1% in 1991 to 12.6% in 1993. In fact, this was the situation faced by many companies in the recessionary period in the UK during that time. Sales were decreasing, or at least not increasing very much in the continuing recession and margins were being squeezed. This is shown very clearly for *Meunier plc* where the sales margin has reduced from 10.8% in 1991 to 5.7% in 1993. On the other hand, sales generation has not decreased. Many companies, in a recession, will take a close look at the assets they hold, in order to increase this ratio to counteract the falling margins ratio.

One other method of reviewing trends that you may encounter is common- size analysis in which the figures in the profit and loss account and the balance sheet are expressed as a percentage of some key figure. The key figure adopted in a common-size profit/loss account is usually sales (or turnover). Shareholders' funds (or capital employed) is the key figure usually adopted in the common-size balance sheets.

Table 2.2   *Meunier plc: Common size consolidated profit and loss accounts for the years ended 31st December*

	1993 %	1992 %	1991 %
Turnover	100.0	100.0	100.0
Cost of sales	*10·17 ≈* 48.3	47.1	43.0
Gross profit	51.7	52.9	57.0
Operating expenses	45.9	45.5	46.2
Operating profit	5.8	7.4	10.8
Interest payable	1.6	2.7	2.1
Profit before tax	4.2	4.7	8.7
Taxation	1.2	1.3	2.7
Profit attributable to shareholders	3.0	3.4	6.0
Dividends	2.6	2.6	2.6
Transfer to reserves	0.4	0.8	3.4

What can be gained from such analysis? Well, if we consider the profit attributable to shareholders in the common size profit and loss account in *Table 2.2*, there was a major decline from 6% to 3.4% between 1991 and 1992, and a smaller decline from 3.4% to 3% between 1992 and 1993. This fall can be seen to be mainly because of increased cost of sales which have risen from 43% in 1991 to 48.3% in 1993. By comparison operating expenses, interest payable, and taxation have fallen.

Table 2.3   *Meunier plc: Common size consolidated balance sheets for the years ended 31st December*

	1993 %	1992 %	1991 %
Fixed assets			
Tangible fixed assets	114.2	115.5	107.4
Current assets			
Stocks	92.5	83.2	80.4
Debtors	46.3	47.3	45.9
Cash	0.4	0.4	0.3
	139.2	130.9	126.6
Creditors: amounts falling due within one year	126.9	105.5	93.7
Net current assets	12.3	25.4	32.9
Total assets less current liabilities	126.5	140.9	140.3
Creditors: amounts falling due after one year	26.5	40.9	40.3
	100.0	100.0	100.0
Capital and reserves			
Called up share capital	18.3	20.0	20.9
Share premium account	51.0	45.9	45.4
Revaluation reserve	2.8	3.2	3.4
Profit and loss account	27.9	30.9	30.3
Shareholders' funds	100.0	100.0	100.0

As regards the common-size balance sheet in *Table 2.3*, current assets and particularly stocks have increased over the three year period, as have creditors amounts falling due within one year. This has had a noticeable effect upon "Net current assets", the difference between current assets and creditors falling due within one year. This can be seen to have fallen from 32.9% in 1991 to 25.4% in 1992, and 12.3% in 1993. In order to look further behind the reason for the increase in such creditors it is necessary to refer to the notes to the accounts. If we focus our attention upon note 3, it reveals an increase in bank borrowings to be a major contributor to the increase in this class of creditors. It also reveals that the loan notes are now close to redemption. These are long-term borrowings which have a finite life, at the end of which have to be repaid. Because they are now close to redemption they have been reclassified from being creditors falling due after one year to creditors falling due within one year.

In our review of strategic analysis in *Chapter 1* the importance of making comparisons with competitors was highlighted. And, the approach we have illustrated for analysing *Meunier's* performance historically can be readily applied to competitors (with the proviso that the necessary data is available). As can be seen in *Table 2.4* , three comparable companies have been identified and are shown as A, B and C:

Table 2.4   *Operating data for Meunier plc and selected comparable companies in the publishing/ bookstores business for the latest 12 months - 1993*

	Meunier plc	A	B	C
1. Sales (turnover) £m	210.6	713.4	312.6	91.7
2. Operating profit (before interest and taxation) £m	12.1	74.9	23.4	8.4
3. Return on sales % $(2 \div 1 \times 100)$	5.7	10.5	7.5	9.2

By comparison with its competitors, *Meunier's* return on sales looks very poor. However, we do have the position relating to one year only. Furthermore, it is difficult to form a more holistic view without looking at the relative sales generation ratios and also RONA. Having done this, if there were still indications of a relative problem as regards return on sales, a more searching analysis of cost ratios would be appropriate [1] .

Corporate level ratio analysis - extending the ratio hierarchy

Our review of ratio analysis for strategic purposes really needs to go much further than our discussions so far which have centred upon RONA and its component ratios. This actually involves moving higher up the hierarchy, or pyramid, to what we will refer to as the *corporate level.*

The example earlier of *GEC* did not include any of the ratios at corporate level, but there are companies who do and/or have quoted such ratios in a fair degree of detail. One good example that we will draw upon frequently and which extends our geographic boundaries beyond the UK is *The Quaker Oats Company*, the US corporation which specialises in grocery products.

As far back as its 1989 Annual Report, *The Quaker Oats Company* illustrates its corporate performance in terms of Return On Equity (ROE) which we reviewed in *Chapter 1* alongside RONA [2]. The company's performance is illustrated in the Annual Report as shown in *Table 2.5*. In this table, the terms we have applied so far and more common UK terms for those we have not encountered are shown in parentheses:

Table 2.5   The Quaker Oats Company performance 1984-1989

Fiscal Years	1984	1985	1986	1987	1988	1989
Asset Turnover						
(Sales Generation)	1.96	1.83	1.78	1.67	1.71	1.85
x						
Return on Net Sales						
(Return On Sales)	4.03%	4.37%	4.76%	4.20%	4.80%	3.55%
=						
Return on Assets						
(Return On Net Assets)	7.90%	8.00%	8.47%	7.01%	8.22%	6.57%
x						
Leverage Factor						
(Gearing)	2.41	2.42	2.40	2.76	2.66	2.59
=						
Return On Equity	19.0%	19.4%	20.3%	19.4%	21.9%	17.0%
Pro forma Return on Equity *	19.0%	19.4%	20.4%	20.4%	22.7%	23.5%

* Assumes all major restructuring charges and accounting changes are excluded each year.

This analysis by *The Quaker Oats Company* illustrates that ROE can be directly related to our earlier RONA analysis. What is more this analysis can be extended yet further as we illustrate in *Figure 2.2*.

Figure 2.2   **Corporate and managerial level ratios**

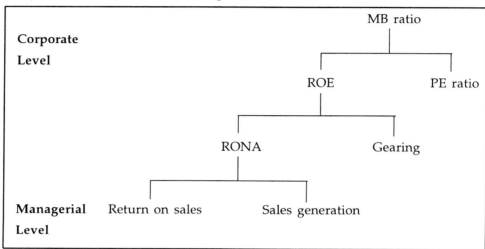

In terms of our example company, *Meunier plc,* we can only calculate ratios up to and including ROE because we have no share price. For the MB (market-to-book) and PE (price-earnings) ratios a share price is essential as you will see shortly. (Please also note that because a company has plc after its name it is not automatically to be assumed to have a stock market quotation. Many companies are plc's without necessarily having any quoted shares.)

So what are these ratios for *Meunier plc?* We have extended *Table 2.1* to illustrate them:

Table 2.6 *Meunier plc: Corporate and managerial level ratios*

Ratios	How to calculate ratios	1993	1992	1991
1. RONA%	c ÷ e x 100 - %	12.6%	15.8%	23.1%
2. Return on sales%	c ÷ d x 100 - %	5.7%	7.4%	10.8%
3. Sales generation	d ÷ e - x (times)	2.2x	2.1x	2.1x
4. ROE%	f ÷ g x 100 - %	8.3%	10.2%	18.1%
5. Gearing	e ÷ g - x (times)	1.3x	1.4x	1.4x
	Where to look	**1993 £m**	**1992 £m**	**1991 £m**
a. Profit before tax	Profit and loss account	8.7	9.4	16.3
b. Interest payable	Note 1 to account	3.4	5.3	3.9
c. Profit before interest and tax	a + b	12.1	14.7	20.2
d. Sales	Profit and loss account (Turnover)	210.6	199.6	187.4
e. Net assets	Balance sheet (total assets less current liabilities)	96.0	93.0	87.4
f. Profit attributable to shareholders	Profit and loss account	6.3	6.7	11.3
g. Shareholders' funds	Balance sheet	75.9	66.0	62.3

Whereas the ratios for *The Quaker Oats Company* fitted together perfectly such that ROE was the product of lower level ratios, this is not so in our *Meunier* illustration. This is because the profit figures used in calculating ROE and RONA are different for a very good reason. The concern in measuring RONA is to examine the profitability generated by the business irrespective of how the business is funded. By comparison, ROE is a measure of the profit that shareholders receive and the profit figure used is therefore after tax and interest have been deducted.

It would be relatively easy to show *Meunier* with the ratios fitting perfectly simply by changing the definition of profit to a measure common to both ROE and RONA calculations, but this is not normal practice.

What about the results shown for *Meunier*? Well the RONA and ROE decline since 1991 certainly warrant an examination, which is where the hierarchy approach becomes particularly useful.   However, within the realms of valuation, which you will remember is our concern in this book, there are other issues that have to be taken into consideration that we will take up in the next chapter. For now, let us review the other ratios in this corporate level hierarchy.

Gearing

Gearing (or leverage in the US) combined with RONA produces ROE. So what is gearing?   Gearing expresses the relationship between some measure of interest-bearing capital and some measure of the equity capital or the total capital employed.   As indicated by the vagueness of this definition, one potential difficulty with gearing is that there are many alternative measures that can be used, hence the reference to "some measure" for both interest-bearing capital and equity capital. For example, from one perspective interest-bearing capital would consist of short and long term bank and institutional loans, finance leases, and preference shares, whilst to other users quite different measures would be applicable, as the following example serves to illustrate. Consider a company with the following results:

1.	Short-term loans	£100m
2.	Long-term loans	£140m
3.	Preference shares	£20m
4.	Ordinary shareholders' funds	£400m
5.	Cash at bank	£114m
6.	Market value of long-term debt	£200m
7.	Market value of shareholders' funds	£1,600m

We can calculate many different gearing ratios using the above data. Given a different perspective one might be preferred to another, but none is necessarily incorrect. The following calculations illustrate what some of these might be:

$$\frac{\text{Long-term loans}}{\text{Total equity (3+4)}} = \frac{£140m}{£420m} = 33.3\%$$

$$\frac{\text{Long-term loans + Preference shares}}{\text{Ordinary shareholders' funds}} = \frac{£160m}{£400m} = 40\%$$

$$\frac{\text{Long-term loans + Short-term loans}}{\text{Ordinary shareholders' funds}} = \frac{£240m}{£400m} = 60\%$$

$$\frac{\text{Long-term loans + Short-term loans - Cash at bank}}{\text{Ordinary shareholders' funds}} = \frac{£126m}{£400m} = 31.5\%$$

$$\frac{\text{Market value of debt}}{\text{Market value of equity}} = \frac{£200m}{£1,600m} = 12.5\%$$

What these different results serve to illustrate is that it in interpreting the results for a particular gearing ratio, it really is important to know how it was defined.

Why is gearing important? A company with a large proportion of net debt to equity is said to be highly geared. The importance of gearing is that in a highly-geared company changes in operating profit may have disproportionate effects on the return accruing to ordinary shareholders. A common view is that beyond some point the return required by the providers of funds will become very high because of a concern about the company's ability to meet servicing costs.

So what is an acceptable level of gearing? The answer is that it all depends upon the economic climate in terms of business confidence as manifested in interest rates, and so on, and the type of business. Businesses with a strong track record, substantial fixed assets that they own and which are not very prone to the ravages of the business cycle can, other things being equal, be more highly geared than others. Given such influences, it is actually very difficult to be definitive about the exact value to place on gearing, but we will review the issue of gearing later in the book when we consider the rate of return required by providers of funds, often known as the cost of capital.

Price-Earnings and Market-to-Book ratios

The last two corporate level ratios in the hierarchy for us to review are the price-earnings (PE) and market-to-book (MB) ratios, which we saw were related as follows:

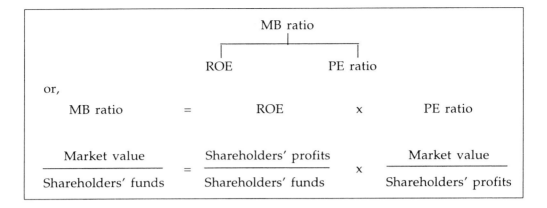

Cancel out shareholders' profits which are common to both ROE and PE and the result is the MB ratio.

We are unable to calculate them for *Meunier* because of there being no publicly quoted share price. But, why are they important and how are they calculated?

Within a valuation context, both the PE and the MB are used to estimate values for companies that are not quoted and also to estimate the values of parts of a quoted company that need valuing. As you will see in the next section, given an shareholders' profits (earnings attributable to shareholders) and shareholders' funds (book value) for a company to be valued, together with representative PE and MB ratios for a peer group, a market price can be estimated.

We have already reviewed ROE and doubtless many of you will at least heard of or read about PE. But what exactly is a PE ratio? The PE ratio is often viewed as one of the most significant indicators of corporate performance and it is widely quoted in the financial press. It is calculated by dividing the market price of a share by the earnings per share (or the total market value by total profit attributable to shareholders), i.e.

$$\text{PE ratio} \quad = \quad \frac{\text{Market price of a share}}{\text{Earnings per share}}$$

The market price of a share is readily available for quoted companies, as is their earnings per share which is required to be reported in their annual accounts.

The PE ratio indicates how much investors are willing to pay for a company's current earnings. Potential high growth companies tend to have high PE ratios, while those with little or no growth have low ratios. However, the PE of a company also depends not only on the company itself, but on the industry in which it operates and, of course, on the level of the stock market, which tends to rise more than reported profits when the business cycle swings up and to fall more than profits in a downturn.

The Actuaries Share Indices table published in the *Financial Times* every day except Mondays also gives the PE ratio for each industry group and subsection, so any historical PE ratio calculated for a company can be compared with its sector and the market as a whole. The result of comparing it with the market as a whole is called the PE Relative:

$$PE\ Relative\ =\ \frac{PE\ of\ the\ company}{PE\ of\ the\ market}$$

This provides a quick indication of whether a company is highly or lowly rated, although differences in the treatment of tax by individual companies do cause some distortions, such that analysts will tend to standardise their calculations.

In general, a high historic PE ratio compared with the industry group suggests either that the company is a leader in its sector or that the share is overvalued, while a low PE ratio suggests a poor company or an undervalued share. It is worthwhile being cautious of companies with very high PE ratios because it may signify a "glamour stock" due for a tumble or, if it is the PE ratio of a very sound high quality company, the market itself may be in for a fall.

Whereas the PE ratio relates shareholders' profits to the market value. The MB ratio expresses the relationship between market value and shareholders' funds. The PE has a direct link with the profit and loss account and the MB has a direct link with the balance sheet.

Figure 2.3   Components of PE and MB ratios

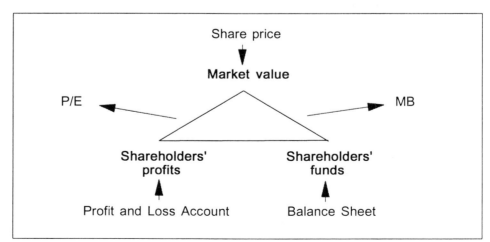

But, can the PE and MB ratios be used in linking finance and strategy? We will consider this in the next section where we review business valuation using peer group analysis.

Peer group analysis

A major challenge in many issues of strategic choice concerns how to value the potential options that are available. For example, if faced with a potential acquisition which is a private company or the division of a publicly quoted company, how can you establish its value? One approach widely used is to apply what is known as peer group analysis, where the financial performance of a number of publicly quoted peers is used in conjunction with key financial information about the company in question.

In this section we will review the application of peer group analysis using the PE and MB ratio approaches. In so doing we will draw upon material covered in the last section and illustrate how it can be applied in this context. We will make use of the information in the Appendix relating to *Meunier plc* and more data relating to companies A, B and C which we introduced earlier to show how the principles can be applied.

Let us first consider the additional data relating to companies A, B and C which is summarised in *Table 2.7*:

Table 2.7   *Operating data (latest 12 months) 1993 for peer group companies*

	Company A	Company B	Company C
1. Sales (turnover) £m	713.4	312.6	91.7
2. Operating profit (before interest and taxation) £m *	74.9	23.4	8.4
3. Return on sales % (2 ÷ 1)	10.5	7.5	9.2
4. Net income (operating profit after interest and taxation) £m	43.1	11.5	8.4
5. Number of shares issued	132.6	43.9	15.7
6. Earnings per share (EPS) (4 ÷ 5)	32.5p	26.2p	53.5p
7. Market price	653p	382p	845p
8. PE ratio (7 ÷ 6)	20.1	14.6	15.8
9. Book value of shareholders' funds £m	276.3	113.9	57.5
10. Book value per share (9 ÷ 5)	208p	259p	366p
11. MB ratio (7 ÷ 10)	3.1	1.5	2.3

*   This figure is also known as Earnings Before Interest and Taxation (EBIT) in some countries.

We will now use this data, together with that relating to Meunier to calculate estimated values. This will involve two steps illustrated in the next two tables. They are:

1 Calculate mean PE and MB ratio values for the three peer group companies excluding Meunier

2 Calculate estimated values for *Meunier* using high, low and mean PE and MB ratio values

Step 1: Calculate mean PE and MB ratios for three peer companies

Figures for peer group companies in the publishing/bookstores business				
	Mean	A	B	C
PE ratio	16.8	20.1	14.6	15.8
MB ratio	2.3	3.1	1.5	2.3

Step 2: Calculate high, mean and low values for *Meunier* using PE and MB ratios for peer group companies, latest 12 months' operating data 1993

	Meunier plc	High	Mean	Low
PE method				
1. Earnings per share	4.53p			
2. PE ratio		20.1	16.8	14.6
Market value of shares (1 x 2)		91p	76p	66p
MB method				
3. Book value per share *	55p			
4. MB ratio		3.1	2.3	1.5
Market value of shares (3 x 4)		171p	127p	83p

* Shareholders' funds from Balance Sheet divided by number of shares (£75.9m ÷ 139m)

The result of using peer group information is a market value per share based upon the PE method ranging from 66p to 91p with a mean of 76p and figures of 83p to 171p with a mean of 127p based upon the MB ratio.

A key issue arises as to what values are the most appropriate to use and, indeed, whether three companies is sufficient. In fact, in our experience those using this approach will often look at a range far greater than high, mean and low estimates, and will also frequently have a sample of peers substantially greater than three companies. Of course, this does not simplify the task of valuation, rather it makes it more difficult.

How given a whole range of potential values can the most appropriate value be found? At this stage it is not unusual to introduce qualitative issues, to our minds making a complex picture even more so. We favour an approach that enables judgements to be integrated within much of the financial analysis. How this can be achieved we review at length in subsequent chapters.

Concluding remarks

We hope that you are feeling somewhat uneasy with this approach, because we certainly are! What concerns us and causes us to have little faith in this approach is that it creates far too much of a "black box" effect. What really is required is an approach which enables all manner of assumptions to be taken into consideration as input data which is then processed in an understandable fashion to produce an output. As you will see in later chapters it is quite possible to remove much of this black box effect to produce far more meaningful valuations. Furthermore, peer group analysis can be used to good effect to assist in the valuation process.

So to summarise, we have shown how ratios can be used for strategic financial analysis and we have identified some limitations to its use, but there are others. What these are we will consider in the next chapter where we review the limitations of accounting-based approaches.

Appendix

Meunier plc:

Consolidated profit and loss accounts for the years ended 31st December

	Notes	1993	1992	1991
		£m	£m	£m
Turnover		210.6	199.6	187.4
Cost of sales		101.8	94.1	80.6
Gross profit		108.8	105.5	106.8
Operating expenses		96.7	90.8	86.6
Operating profit		12.1	14.7	20.2
Interest payable	1	3.4	5.3	3.9
Profit before tax		8.7	9.4	16.3
Taxation		2.4	2.7	5.0
Profit attributable to shareholders		6.3	6.7	11.3
Dividends		5.5	5.2	4.9
Transfer to reserves		0.8	1.5	6.4
Earnings per share		4.53		

Meunier plc:

Consolidated balance sheets for the years ended 31st December

	Notes	1993 £m	1992 £m	1991 £m
Fixed assets				
Tangible fixed assets		86.7	76.2	66.9
Current assets				
Stocks		70.2	54.9	50.1
Debtors	2	35.1	31.2	28.6
Cash		0.3	0.3	0.2
		105.6	86.4	78.9
Creditors: amounts falling due within one year	3	96.3	69.6	58.4
Net current assets		9.3	16.8	20.5
Total assets less current liabilities		96.0	93.0	87.4
Creditors: amounts falling due after one year	3	20.1	27.0	25.1
		75.9	66.0	62.3
Capital and reserves				
Called up share capital (10p shares)	4	13.9	13.2	13.0
Share premium account		38.7	30.3	28.3
Revaluation reserve		2.1	2.1	2.1
Profit and loss account		21.2	20.4	18.9
Shareholders' funds		75.9	66.0	62.3

Notes to the accounts

	1993 £m	1992 £m	1991 £m
1. **Interest payable**			
Bank borrowings and other loans repayable within 5 years	2.6	4.2	3.3
Finance leases	0.6	0.5	0.3
Hire purchase and sundry loans	0.2	0.6	0.3
	3.4	5.3	3.9
2. **Debtors:** amounts falling due within one year:			
Trade debtors	26.7	25.9	24.3
Other debtors, prepayments and accrued income	8.4	5.3	4.3
	35.1	31.2	28.6
3. **Creditors:** amounts falling due within one year:			
Bank borrowings	24.4	16.0	28.0
Loan notes	12.0	0.0	0.0
Trade creditors	26.7	24.3	16.4
Bills of exchange	3.2	0.2	0.9
Taxation and social security	5.4	7.2	3.1
Finance leases	1.6	2.5	1.3
Hire purchase creditors	4.2	3.6	1.8
Other creditors	7.5	2.4	0.8
Accruals and deferred income	7.8	10.1	3.1
Proposed dividend	3.5	3.3	3.0
	96.3	69.6	58.4

	1993	1992	1991
	£m	£m	£m
Creditors: amounts falling due after one year:			
Loan notes	-	12.0	12.0
Bank and other loans	5.6	2.2	3.6
Finance leases	1.8	1.5	1.2
Hire purchase creditors	7.6	6.8	4.2
Other creditors	4.9	4.3	4.0
Accruals deferred income	0.2	0.2	0.1
	20.1	27.0	25.1

4. Called up share capital

Ordinary shares 10p each. 1993, 139 million (*1992, 132 million*)

References

1. This is beyond the scope of this book, but is covered in Mills R.W. and Robertson J., Fundamentals of Managerial Accounting and Finance, 3rd Edition, Mars Business Associates, 1993, Chapter 3 pp. 73 -105. This chapter also includes a review of the use of total assets as well as net assets in ROCE calculations.

2. The Quaker Oats Company Annual Report, 1989.

3

Accounting, Cash Flow and Business Valuation

> *"Accounting tricks 'fool City analysts'"*
>
> *Andrew Jack*

Introduction

Research conducted at the end of 1990 on 63 experienced investment analysts at five City stock brokers showed that just a handful could see through the most elementary forms of creative accounting in a test of their scrutiny of financial statements [1].

Financial statements like the profit and loss and balance sheet form a core everyday business language and may, therefore, quite naturally appear to be suitable for evaluating longer term strategic plans. However, what the study of investment analysts illustrates is that there may well be significant interpretative problems. Some of these problems may emanate from accounting tricks, but one other problem with financial statements and accounting data in general is that they are based upon accounting conventions and practices which are not necessarily appropriate for strategic financial analysis.

In this chapter we will review the issue of accounting tricks, or *creative accounting* as it is generally known, together with shortcomings of accounting for purposes of strategic financial analysis. Thereafter, we will make the case for using cash flow analysis rather than accounting approaches for strategic financial analysis, and in particular business valuation. Last, but by no means least, we will provide a brief introduction to the Shareholder Value Analysis approach which builds upon cash flow analysis and draws upon the key concepts in finance we outlined in *Chapter 1*.

Creative accounting

Creative accounting has feature strongly in the UK press, particularly with the publication of *Terry Smith's* book in 1992 which was somewhat controversially entitled, "Accounting for growth: how to strip the camouflage from company accounts" [2]. *Smith* demonstrated a number of approaches by which companies could use and had used considerable judgement to produce results which put them in the best possible light, whilst staying within the letter of the law.

However, creative accounting is not a phenomenon of the 1990s and was recognised before the demise of companies like *Polly Peck* which really brought the issue to the fore [3].

Shortly we will review what is meant by creative accounting, but for now let us put the issue in context as regards the concern of this book. A major challenge exists in undertaking meaningful analysis to support strategic decisions. As we illustrated in the last chapter, ratios may be and are used for this purpose, *but the ratios can only be as good as the quality of the data upon which they are based.*

It is our belief that all too often ratio analysis is applied without questioning the quality of the underlying data, a view supported by the study mentioned in the introduction. It found that of 1,325 possible corrections that the 63 experienced investment analysts could have made in calculating financial ratios from a set of accounts full of "window dressing", just 34 adjustments were made in total. What is more, 52 analysts made no corrections at all!

Earlier we made reference to the demise of *Polly Peck*. This actually provides a specific example of the problem highlighted in the study, because just prior to its demise a number of City analysts are reported as having circulated reports recommending that clients buy shares in *Polly Peck International* at the current price of 260p. By all accounts, the authors of these reports predicted a substantial improvement in pre-tax profits for 1990 and 1991. But, just six days later, *Polly Peck*, the conglomerate controlled by *Mr Asil Nadir*, saw its shares plummet to 108p before they were suspended on the Stock Exchange.

A recent book by *Pijper* [4] identifies how in principle a skilled reader of the *Polly Peck* accounts could have seen the troubles afoot. Nevertheless, the plain fact of the matter is that most did not and that there is some evidence to support concerns about the ability of analysts to detect creative accounting problems. So how do companies apply creative accounting and why do they account creatively?

How have companies created a favourable picture of their performance? There are a number of well documented issues associated with creative accounting, such as capitalising interest, brand accounting, acquisition write-downs, extending the time period for accounting for depreciation, and so on. These terms may sound like an accountant's jargon, but think of many of them as being legitimate means by which earnings per share can be all too readily inflated. How? Well, for example, by overlooking and/or understating costs so that they are excluded in the earnings used to calculate earnings per share.

Why do companies account creatively? Well one view that provides some understanding of the likely source of the problem is that the City has been infatuated with earnings per share and the resultant PE ratio. As a consequence the message that the institutional investor delivered to the managers of companies was often crystal clear - produce earnings per share growth, above all else, and your shares will go up. For example, in terms of the valuation exercise we undertook for *Meunier plc* in the last chapter, any action that could be taken to increase earnings per share would increase the estimated share price using the PE ratios for peer group companies.

There are many ways in which the information provided by a company can be seen as helping to provide a more favourable picture. Let us draw upon the last chapter and consider the effects of creative accounting with reference to the PE and MB ratios.

As regards the PE ratio many companies in response to the perceived requirements of their shareholders endeavour to ensure steady growth in their earnings per share. Unfortunately, it is possible to show an improvement in earnings per share by simply influencing the numerator and/or the denominator involved in its calculation without there being any real improvement in performance [5]. Some ways in which this can be achieved are all too obvious, however others may be difficult to detect, even for professional analysts!

One approach that can be used to keep costs away from the profit and loss account is by capitalising them. This is achieved by combining them with fixed assets legitimately and including them in the balance sheet. This is possible because accounting makes a distinction between costs which expire during an accounting period and are written off through the profit and loss account, and assets which do not expire during a single accounting period, and are "held over". If a case can be made for such items to be treated as assets, typically that part which expires during an accounting period will be matched as a cost, the remainder being held in the balance sheet as an asset.

Items often found to be capitalised include:

- ○ Interest
- ○ Research and development
- ○ Start-up costs

To understand how the capitalisation of costs works, consider the extreme case of a company which, after charging interest payable of £8 million through the profit and loss account, makes a loss of £4 million. If this company did not include this interest payable in its profit and loss account, the £4 million loss would be £4 million profit. The £8 million interest payable being included with the fixed assets. The adjustment from a £4 million loss to a £4 million profit can be demonstrated quite simply by adding back interest payable as follows:

Profit and Loss Account	
	£m
Loss	4
Interest payable	8
Profit	4

Such action does not mean that the balance sheet will not balance. Whilst the Net Assets section increases by £8 million so also does the Shareholders' Funds side because the loss of £4 million has changed to a profit of the same amount - a change of £8 million. This is reflected in the retained profit in the profit and loss account which is transferred to the revenue reserves (often referred to as the profit and loss account) in the balance sheet.

Increase in Balance sheet figures	£m
Fixed assets (including capitalised interest)	+ 8
Net assets	+ 8
Profit and loss account (interest excluded)	+ 8
Shareholders' funds	+ 8

When and why do companies capitalise interest costs? The practice may often be used, and not unreasonably, for a large project when the interest is considered to be an indistinguishable part of the cost of an asset.

As illustrated, the effect of capitalisation is often very beneficial to the current year's profit but this may not be quite as much as just illustrated. Why? Because often the interest payable now included within fixed assets will be depreciated together with the actual asset. For example, we will assume that our company with interest payable of £8 million incurs this in relation to a project with a planned timescale of 4 years. Depreciating this sum over 4 years means a reduction in profits for each year of £2 million, assuming a straight-line write-off. The effect is therefore to defer the cost, unless the item never makes an appearance in the profit and loss account - a practice that has been associated with the treatment of investment properties by companies in the property sector.

Whilst capitalising interest can improve earnings per share, and hence the PE ratio, there are measures that can be adopted that will improve shareholders' funds and, therefore, perhaps value if one takes an MB perspective. Let us look at how this might be achieved via brand accounting which became newsworthy in the corporate take-over frenzy of the 1980s, particularly among companies possessing strong, frequently international, brand names.

The debate first really attracted attention in 1988. First, when the Swiss foods conglomerate *Nestlé* bid for control of *Rowntree*, offering more than twice *Rowntree's* pre-bid capitalisation. Second, later that year *Grand Metropolitan* decided to capitalise brands acquired since 1985. Third, and most significantly, *Ranks Hovis McDougall (RHM)* the UK food manufacturing company, now a part of the *Tomkins Group*, moved to capitalise not only acquired, but also internally developed brands.

As a consequence of a valuation of home grown brands by the consultancy, Interbrand, £678m, or approximately one and a half times the value of *RHM's* tangible net assets, was put on the company's balance sheet for brand names [6]. The approach taken by *RHM* and *Interbrand* in capitalising the company's brands was to measure "brand profitability" and to apply a multiple in the form of "brand strength". In a press release by *RHM* on 16 January 1989 the company identified that the brand profit used was that which resulted from the brand's identity. This brand profit, after tax, was a weighted average over a three year period.

In the case of brand strength it was determined as a result of a detailed review of each brand in terms of its positioning, the market in which it operates, competition, past performance, future plans, risks to the brand, and so on. These characteristics were captured in a composite of the following seven weighted factors:

1. Leadership

2. Stability

3. Market vulnerability or volatility

4. Internationality

5. Trend over a long time period

6. Support from investment

7. Protection by trademarks or law

In accounting terms the brand accounting exercise was quite simply achieved by classifying brands of £678m as an intangible asset and balancing this with an entry for reserves under shareholders' funds of the same amount. The effect of such action was dramatic upon a company's balance sheet and perceived level of gearing in terms of the historical book values shown in the financial statements. Furthermore, taking an MB perspective it might be inferred that by increasing shareholders' funds by such an amount the market value of the company should increase. However, a vast change in the company's market value was not the result. Why, if markets are efficient there is good reason to believe that the value of the brands will already have been taken into consideration by the market.

There may be many reasons for undertaking a brand valuation exercise along the lines adopted by *RHM*. However, if the purpose is associated with strategic analysis there is a preferred approach for looking at brands that we will consider in a later section in this chapter with reference to *The Quaker Oats Company*. This company, also in the food manufacturing business, was pursuing an approach at this time focusing upon the cash generative ability of its brands [7]. The substance of this approach has been well reflected in its annual reports since 1988 and we will review it in the last section of this chapter.

The international dimension

It has been estimated that investors worldwide ploughed an estimated $170 billion into foreign equity markets during 1993. Whilst the US was the largest single investor, the bulk of the cross border flows originated from Europe. One in every five shares traded worldwide is now estimated to involve either a foreign share or a foreign investor by comparison to only one in fourteen during the late 1970s [8].

The international dimension is not only a feature of the investing community, but also of strategic initiatives by corporations. You only have to think of the recent acquisition of *Rover* cars by *BMW* and the Japanese involvement by *Honda* to appreciate this point.

How does this international dimension impact upon our storyline so far? Well, not only are there problems of creative accounting that need to be taken into consideration, but also some other difficulties in working with accounting based measures that need to be brought into the discussion. These difficulties can be seen if we take a more international perspective. They have been well illustrated in a number of studies of the European Community where, unlike many other parts of the world, a "harmonisation" of accounting and financial reporting practices has been under way.

Harmonisation is a term that is frequently misunderstood. It is all too easy to view it as implying the adoption of identical practices rather than its typical consequence - compromise. The effect of harmonisation of accountancy practices in the EC was brought out in a study by *Touche Ross* [9].

Members of *Touche Ross* in seven EC states were asked to prepare accounts (in ECU) for the *same* hypothetical group of companies, thus providing statements which should be directly comparable as between different jurisdictions. For the profit and loss account participants were asked to use the maximum flexibility of local rules, to provide three alternative figures

1. that which a real company would be most likely to arrive at

2. the highest profit possible, and

3. the lowest profit possible.

The results of the study summarised in *Table 3.1* are interesting to say the least!

Table 3.1   EC profit differences

	ECU millions		
	Most Likely Net Profit	Maximum Net Profit	Minimum Net Profit
Belgium	135	193	90
Germany	133	**140**	27
Spain	131	192	121
France	149	160	121
Italy	174	193	167
Netherlands	140	156	76
United Kingdom	192	194	**171**

The results of the study illustrate the potential for significant differences in reported net profits between European Community (EC) member states. Also that the range over which the profit may be measured could be different. To take extreme cases, the British profit could have been at worst 171m ECU while the German profit could have been at best 140m ECU.

A major reason for the difference between the net profit figures concerns the treatment of goodwill, taxation, and stocks. For example, goodwill can be written-off immediately against reserves, or amortised over a number of future years profits. Within the European Community it is only in the UK that the immediate write-off of goodwill against reserves in the balance sheet is the most popular practice. In other member states and the USA goodwill is normally written off against future profits, with the number of years against which it is amortised varying from country to country, as can be seen below:

	Amortisation Period
Belgium	5 years
Germany	15 years
France	20 years
Italy	10 years
Netherlands	10 years
USA	40 years (up to)

The impact of these differences are illustrated in *Table 3.2*, where goodwill purchased of £400 million has been accounted for according to these different amortisation periods.

Table 3.2   *Accounting treatment for goodwill*

		Belgium £m	USA £m	France £m	UK £m
A	Profit attributable to ordinary shareholders	100	100	100	100
B	Goodwill purchased	400	400	400	400
C	Number of years	5	40	20	0
D	Amortisation of goodwill (B ÷ C)	80	10	20	-
E	Adjusted profit (A - D)	20	90	80	100
F	Number of shares	200	200	200	200
	Earnings per share (E ÷ F)	10p	45p	40p	50p

As you can see, the different treatment of goodwill has a significant impact upon adjusted profit and earnings per share.

The implication of such differences is that you do have to be very careful in interpreting the reported performance of companies from different countries. One important way of understanding whether there are differences is the accounting policies published within annual reports. A comparison of these for two companies from different countries will often reveal differences in accounting practices.

Global harmonisation initiatives are under way in the attempt to remove significant differences in accounting and financial reporting practices. However, a lack of strong professional accountancy bodies in certain countries makes the notion of global harmonisation appear to be idealistic. A second problem is nationalism, which may show itself in an unwillingness to accept compromises that involve changing accounting practices to match those of other countries. This unwillingness may arise on the part of accountants and companies, or Member States that do not wish to lose their sovereignty.

Moves towards global harmonisation are being encouraged by multinational companies. This was indicated in an update of a survey published in 1992 of 206 European companies with multiple stock exchange listings [10]. It reviewed the 1990 annual reports in various languages of a number of major European companies whose international financial reporting practises had been found to be particularly innovative in one or more respects. The main features of the transnational reports studied were:

❍ Adapting communication to meet different audiences. For example, *Volkswagen's* 1990 annual report was published in English, German, Chinese, French, Italian, Japanese, Portuguese, Slovakian, Spanish and Czech. A condensed version of the 1990 annual report was also available in Polish, Russian and Hungarian.

❍ Convenience currency translation. This refers to the restatement of financial statement items from the main reporting currency into one or more other currencies thought to be more convenient either for particular groups of readers or for particular reporting purposes, with a view to enhancing the cross-sectional comparability of the information. (These convenience currency translations are of a voluntary nature and need to be distinguished from the currency translations which are a necessary part of the process of preparing consolidated financial statements of multinational groups.)

But the key question arises, has global harmonisation really moved forwards? A survey by *Emenyonu and Gray* in 1993 aimed to assess progress in the last 25 years [11]. They studied 293 companies reporting in both 1971/2 and 1991/2 drawn from five countries - France, Germany, Japan, the UK and the USA.

In view of the size and significance of these companies and the importance of the countries involved, we might expect that the impact of efforts to harmonise accounting internationally would be clearly discernible. Furthermore, as the researchers acknowledge, this is the kindest sample to choose. A much tougher test of harmonisation would be to look far more globally and to include both large and small companies, listed and unlisted.

Emenyonu and Gray highlighted a total of 26 accountancy measurement issues and constructed a "harmony index" for each. This index provides a range of values from zero for extreme diversity to one for an absolute uniformity of accounting methods. They found that using this measure, progress towards harmonisation over the last 20 years has been mixed. There were only 14 issues showing an increase in harmonisation and, in fact, in 12 cases there was a reduction in harmonisation or a higher level of accounting diversity.

Taken overall, harmonisation has been quite modest, with an increase in the average harmony index score from a moderate level of 0.6230 to only 0.6903. This is an average increase in international accounting harmonisation of only 10.8 per cent from 1971/2 to 1991/2.

Thus, from a large company perspective, and especially those with multiple stock exchange listings, international harmonisation of accounting and financial reporting is making mixed progress. On the positive side this may be due in part to the effects of the European Community Directives which, although leaving a number of gaps and having some of the shortcomings, do have an impact beyond the ambit of the existing community of twelve. This is quite simply because a number of other countries are now planning to join the European Community and are thus anticipating the need to comply with the directives.

We should also not overlook many large multinationals who may wish to project the image that their financial reporting meets the highest of international standards, and their annual reports including financial reporting practices form part of the strategy of financial public relations. This may be coupled with the fact that they frequently have to produce financial statements which meet the requirements of stock exchanges in more than one country (e.g. the US and UK) and/or countries that have aligned some of their financial reporting requirements on the standards of the International Accounting Standards Committee (IASC). Whilst there are some areas of financial reporting in which considerable progress has been made, there are others where quite the opposite has been the case, and much remains to be done.

For our purposes in this book, traditional accounting-based measures are deficient because they may not fully reveal all the implications associated with pursuing a future course of action. Our concern is also that we need a means of measuring future performance over time rather than at a specific point in time. As we will demonstrate, longer term perspective of performance analysis can be achieved by the use of a net present value type approach. The impact of the various contributors to the value of a business can be included taking into account their future contributions to the business as well as their results from the past.

Shortcomings of accounting numbers

A number of shortcomings of accounting numbers in failing to measure changes in the economic value of the firm have long been recognised [12]. Earnings in particular have been identified as having very significant shortcomings that can be attributed to the following reasons:

1. Alternative accounting methods may be employed.
2. Risk is excluded.
3. Investment requirements are excluded.
4. The time value of money is ignored

As we will demonstrate, these shortcomings can overcome by using a cash flow approach that relies upon a principle known as discounting, which we review in the next chapter. But, are there any other benefits associated with using cash flow and does it really seem to offer any advantages over and above accounting-based approaches? Let us now turn to consider these questions.

The importance of cash

"CASH IS KING"

"There is no substitute for cash generation........   ....There are other things in business life, but nothing is quite so important."

The Treasurer [13]

There is little doubt that the recent UK recession focused attention very clearly upon cash flow. But, does cash flow analysis convey any real benefits as far as strategic analysis is concerned. Certainly some analysts believe so. For example, *UBS Phillips and Drew*, in a publication called "Accounting for Growth" which preceded *Terry Smith's* controversial book of a similar name, argued that playing creative accounting games with profits is relatively easy, but cash flow is the most difficult parameter to adjust in a company's accounts [14]. Furthermore, and perhaps more importantly, it was argued that tracing cash movements in a company *can often lead to the identification of unusual accounting practices.*

The view was also expressed in "Accounting for Growth" that long term return of an equity investment is determined by the market's perception of the stream of dividends that the company will be able to pay. Consequently, less emphasis should be placed on the reported progression of earnings per share and more attention paid to balance sheet movements, dividend potential and, most importantly of all, cash.

But, is there anything to substantiate the claimed superiority of cash over conventional accounting measures? Well, a considerable amount of empirical research has demonstrated that there is a significant relationship between cash flow and share prices. This is particularly so when cash flow is measured in terms of those cash flows to and from long-term lenders and shareholders [15-24]. For example, *Bowen, Burgstahler and Daley* in a US study published 1987 found that cash flow information has incremental explanatory power beyond that contained in accounting measures flows alone. *Arnold, Clubb, Manson and Wearing* confirmed this finding using UK data in a study published in 1991.

As well as research confirming the superiority of cash flow measures over conventional accounting measures, specific accounting based indicators of performance have been found in recent UK studies to fare poorly as measures of shareholder return, that is what shareholders expect to receive by way of dividends and capital appreciation. For example, in a study reported in 1988 *Michael Barron and John Lawless* found that there is, overall, only a modest statistical relationship between shareholder return and earnings per share growth and virtually no relationship at all with return on equity [24]. This was confirmed by *Dennis Henry and Geoff Smith of P-E International*. In their work, based upon a sample of 250 largest UK industrial and commercial companies over a five year period, they found *no* correlation at all between earnings per share and shareholder return [25].

You may find it surprising that earnings per share, so often presented as being a major indicator of corporate performance fares so poorly. How is it that there is such a poor relationship between earnings per share and shareholder return? A major source of the problem as far as the UK is concerned can be attributed to the creative accounting practices we reviewed earlier, but there are the other shortcomings associated with accounting numbers identified by *Rappaport*.

With the shortcomings of accounting numbers in mind and the relative advantage of cash flow, let us consider how cash flow can be developed into a model for strategic analysis. Our starting point will be the Shareholder Value Analysis approach developed by *Rappaport* which we review in the next section.

Shareholder Value Analysis [26]

Shareholder Value Analysis is a framework which addresses many of the shortcomings of accounting-based approaches and accounting numbers. This financial framework can be seen to be particularly appropriate for dealing with strategic issues where those involved need to understand how many diverse aspects of their business can be drawn together and expressed meaningfully in financial terms.

The fundamental assumption in Shareholder Value Analysis is that in broad terms the value of a business can be determined by discounting its future cash flows using an appropriate cost of capital and it provides a framework for understanding and measuring the ramifications of all types of strategic decisions.

There are many features of this approach which makes it seem very much like the net present value model we review at length in the next chapter which has long been used in evaluating capital projects. Indeed it has many similarities insofar as it draws upon the principles of discounted cash flow analysis, but it has some additional features that makes it distinctive.

As we will demonstrate, the framework as structured allows trade-offs like the immediate cash flows associated with significant capital investment to be weighed up against longer term cash flows. These are captured via a number of what are known as *value drivers.*

There are seven basic value drivers which can be expanded and analysed in far more detail. This is often so in real life situations, but the concern here is to demonstrate the integrative and holistic nature of the Shareholder Value Analysis framework. These seven value drivers are

1. Sales growth rate
2. Operating profit margin
3. Cash tax rate
4. Fixed capital investment
5. Working capital investment
6. Planning period
7. Cost of capital

As we will show in subsequent chapters, cash flows within the model are determined by focusing upon the first five value drivers which can be divided into two groups corresponding with decisions about managing operations and investment within a business. The first group of value drivers consisting of sales growth rate, operating profit margin and cash tax rate is instrumental in determining cash inflows. The second consisting of fixed and working capital investment is instrumental in determining cash outflows. The difference between these two represents what is known as *free cash flow.*

Free cash flow recognises the long-term implications associated with short-term actions. It need not be and may not be positive. For example, in a start-up situation, or when introducing a new product significant fixed and working capital investment may well be required. Of course, such investments in fixed and working capital may often represent a significant drain on immediate cash flow. But, the intention in incurring such expenditure will be to benefit from a larger cash flow from operations in the future than would otherwise be the case. In other words long-term value is intended to be driven from a decision with immediate implications. Similarly, a decision not to invest in such a situation will yield higher immediate cash flows but is likely to generate less in the future.

Concluding remarks

Are approaches like Shareholder Value Analysis being used in practice ? The answer is increasingly, yes. Quite how we will review later. For now let us just relate the application of Shareholder Value Analysis to one issue we reviewed, brand valuation.

We made brief reference to the approach adopted towards brands by *The Quaker Oats Company*, the US food manufacturer. Whilst the 1989 Annual Report and Accounts for *Ranks Hovis McDougall* was noteworthy for its approach to accounting for brands, *The Quaker Oats Company's* was heavily oriented towards the importance of cash flow analysis. It demonstrated using the value driver approach how sales growth, operating profit margin and investment have been used to evaluate the value potential of the company taking a long-term cash generative perspective [27].

In fact, *The Quaker Oats Company* has long used the Shareholder Value Analysis approach and has communicated this in numerous annual reports. But, what does this approach really entail, and if future cash flows are so important how do you estimate them? These are some of the questions we will answer in the chapters which follow.

References

1. Jack A., "Accounting tricks 'fool City analysts'", Financial Times, December 8, 1993, p 24.

2. Smith T., *Accounting for Growth: Stripping the camouflage from company accounts*, Century Business, 1992.

3. Griffith I., *Creative Accounting: How to make your profits what you want them to be*, Unwin Hyman, 1986.

4. Pijper T., *Creative Accounting: The effectiveness of financial reporting in the UK*, MacMillan, 1994.

5. Earnings per share calculations in the UK were a source of considerable concern and it is worth noting that the potential for many creative accounting endeavours has been reduced as a result of the implementation of Financial Reporting Standard (FRS) 3 by the Accounting Standards Board. Via this standard earnings per share is calculated on profit attributable to equity shareholders *after* minority interest, extraordinary items, preference dividends and other appropriations in respect of preference shares have been deducted.

6. Ranks Hovis McDougall plc, Annual Report and Accounts, 1989.

7. The Quaker Oats Company, Annual Report, 1989.

8. Riley, B., "Funds Pour into New Growth Regions, Emerging Markets: Financial Times Survey", Monday, February 7, 1994, page 1.

9. Simmonds A. and Azieres O., "Accounting for Europe: success by 2000 AD?", Touche Ross, 1989.

10. Archer S. and McLeay S., "European financial reporting", in *Student Financial Reporting 1991-1992: A Guide to UK Reporting Practice for Accountancy Students*, The Institute of Chartered accountants in England and Wales, 1992.

11. Emenyonu E. and Gray S., "Elusive harmony", Financial Times Accountancy Column, Thursday July 1, 1993, p 9.

12. Rappaport A., *Creating Shareholder Value - The New Standard for Business Performance*, The Free Press, 1986.

13. "Cash Is King", The Treasurer, October, 1991.

14. UBS Phillips and Drew, "Accounting for Growth", 1991.

15. Bowen R. M., Burgstahler D. and Daley L. A., "Evidence on the Relationships Between Earnings and Various Measures of Cash Flow", The Accounting Review, LXI (4), 1986, pp.713-725.

16. Gombola M. J. and Ketz J. E.,"A Note on Cash Flow and Classification Patterns of Financial Ratios", The Accounting Review, LVIII(1), 1983, pp. 105-115.

17. Rayburn J., "The Association of Operating Cash Flow and Accruals with Security Returns", Journal of Accounting Research, 24, 1986, Supplement, pp. 112-133.

18. Wilson G. P., "The Relative Information Content of Accruals and Cash Flows: Combined Evidence at the Earnings Announcement and Annual Report Release Date", Journal of Accounting Research, 1986, 24, Supplement, pp. 165-200.

19. Wilson G. P., "The Incremental Information Content of the Accrual and Funds Components of Earnings After Controlling for Earnings", The Accounting Review, LXII(2), 1987, pp. 293-322.

20. Bowen R. M., Burgstahler D. and Daley L. A., "The Incremental Information Content of Accrual Versus Cash Flows", The Accounting Review, LXII(4), 1987, pp. 723-747.

21. Bernard V. L. and Stober T. L., The Nature and Amount of Information in Cash Flow and Accruals", The Accounting Review, LXIV(4), 1989, pp. 624-652.

22. Charitou A. G. and Ketz E., "An Empirical Examination of Cash Flow Measures", ABACUS, 27(1), 1991, pp. 51-64.

23. Arnold A. J. Clubb C. D. B. Manson S. and Wearing R. T., "The Relationship between Earnings, Funds Flows and Cash Flows: Evidence for the UK", Accounting and Business Research, Vol. 22, No. 85, pp. 13-19, 1991.

24. Barron M. and Lawless J., "Growth of No Account", Business Magazine, September, 1988.

25. Henry D. and Smith G., Letter to Financial Times, Financial Times, June 27, 1991.

26. Rappaport A., *Creating Shareholder Value - The New Standard for Business Performance*, The Free Press, 1986, Chapter 2.

27. The Quaker Oats Annual Report, 1989, page 23.

4

Evaluating
Strategic Investment Opportunities

> *DCF (Discounted Cash Flow)? It is a new type of jumbo jet, isn't it?*
>
> *Anon.*

Introduction

We have introduced the Shareholder Value Analysis approach which emphasises the use of Discounted Cash Flow (DCF) principles and we made brief reference to its accepted use in evaluating capital projects. In this chapter we will demonstrate how DCF principles can be used in evaluating the potential economic viability of a strategic investment opportunity. However, there are alternative DCF techniques. What is the difference between them and does it matter which approach is used? Are there any issues associated with their use in practice? What is the link between such techniques and business value analysis? These are some of the important issues we will consider in this chapter.

Discounted Cash Flow (DCF) techniques

In this section we will consider the two main DCF techniques:

○ Net Present Value (NPV)

○ Internal Rate of Return (IRR)

The advantages and disadvantages of these two alternative approaches are best illustrated using financial data. Therefore, let us consider the following example involving a choice having to be made of one investment opportunity from a short list of three:

Table 4.1   Financial data relating to three investment proposals

	Proposal 1 £m	Proposal 2 £m	Proposal 3 £m
Cash outlay (now)	54	45	65
Net cash inflows: *			
Year 1	18	21	30
Year 2	18	18	30
Year 3	18	12	30
Year 4	18	19	11**
Year 5	18	15**	
Year 6	18**		

*   Net cash inflows equals annual cash inflows less annual cash outflows.

**   Residual value from liquidating assets has been included in the cash flow
for the final year.

The two DCF techniques NPV and IRR are reliant upon a principle, not illustrated in *Table 4.1*, which involves *discounting*, or *scaling-down*, future cash flows. Essentially, where a potential opportunity involves an outlay in the anticipation of future cash inflows, discounted cash flow analysis is appropriate. However, let us place discounting in context by comparing it with a concept all of us should be familiar with from everyday life, compounding.

Compounding, discounting and present value

The principles of compound interest have long been used to illustrate that £1 received today is not the same as £1 received in the future. For example, given the choice between £1 today or £1 in one year's time, we would not be indifferent, given a rate of interest of 10%.   In these circumstances, our choice would be between £1 today and £1 plus 10p - the appropriate interest on £1 for one year at 10% per annum. The further one goes into the future, the greater will be the requirement to be compensated for interest foregone because of the effect of compounding. So, for example, at the end of two years given a rate of interest of 10%, the choice would be between £1 and £1.21.

In the case of compounding we seek to find a future value given a present value, a time period, and an interest rate. The result of compounding will be affected by the period over which compounding occurs and the rate of interest and can be calculated   using the following formula, where n represents the time period:

Future value = Present value $(1 + \text{Rate of interest})^n$

Whereas this calculation will tell us a future value given the present value, the rate of interest and the time period, this is not appropriate for answering questions about the potential economic benefit associated with many strategic decisions. In their case, what we need to be able to do is understand whether a sum receivable at some time in the future is worthwhile in terms of value today. For this the principle of *discounting* is required, which is the converse of compounding.

In fact, the value today, known as the *present value*, can be readily found if the future value and the rate of interest are known. For example, with a known future value of £1, a time period (n) of one year and an annual rate of interest of 10%, the present value can be found by re-arranging the formula:

Future value	=	Present value $(1 + \text{Rate of interest})^n$
Present value	=	Future value $\div (1 + \text{Rate of interest})^n$
	=	$£1 \div (1.10)^1$
	=	£0.909

Given a time period of two years and annual compound interest of 10% per annum, the present value would be:

Present value	=	Future value $\div (1 + \text{Rate of interest})^n$
	=	$£1 \div (1.10)^2$
	=	$£1 \div (1.10)(1.10)$
	=	£0.826

Present value analysis represents a means by which future values can be converted into comparable present day terms using the discounting principle. Quite simply, a future sum to be received which includes compound interest can be expressed in relative terms to £1 today. Is there any need to calculate present and future values? The answer is no. Tables are widely available to facilitate this task.

Combining cash flow analysis and the time value of money within the DCF framework we are able to evaluate decisions with long-term future implications. However, there is more than just one DCF approach and as we have indicated the two main techniques associated with it are the net present value (NPV) and the internal rate of return (IRR). How they differ we will consider with reference to the *Figure 4.1*:

Figure 4.1   Illustration of cash flows associated with an investment proposal

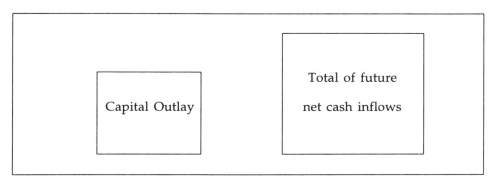

The capital outlay required by the potential investment opportunity is shown alongside the total of future net cash inflows in *Figure 4.1*. The two are not comparable because the total future net cash inflows have not been discounted. So let us review the two approaches, NPV and IRR to see how they would be applied in evaluating a situation like this.

Net Present Value (NPV)

The calculation of NPV involves discounting future net cash inflows to a gross present value and then deducting the capital outlay. For example, in Figure 4.2, NPV equals gross present value minus the capital outlay.

Figure 4.2 Linking cash flows and value - positive NPV

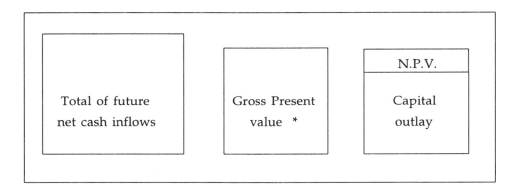

*   Gross present value = sum of discounted future net cash inflows

Where the sum total of discounted future cash flows exceeds the capital outlay the NPV is positive. In this case, illustrated in *Figure 4.2*, the project is acceptable on economic grounds. Conversely, if a negative NPV results where the capital outlay exceeds the gross present value, as illustrated in *Figure 4.3*, the project is not acceptable on economic grounds.

Figure 4.3 Linking cash flows and value - negative NPV

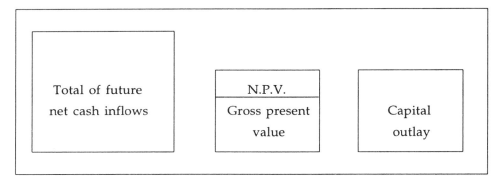

NPV illustration

We will now illustrate the application of the NPV technique using the data for the three potential investment opportunities outlined earlier. Assuming a 10% cost of capital, the net present value for Proposal 1 is calculated as shown in *Table 4.2*.

Table 4.2   NPV - Calculation of Proposal 1

Year	Column 1 Discounted Cash Flow Factor 10%	Column 2 Cash Flows £m	Column 3 (Col. 1 x Col. 2) Present Value £m	
1	0.909	18	16.362	
2	0.826	18	14.868	
3	0.751	18	13.518	
4	0.683	18	12.294	
5	0.621	18	11.178	
6	0.564	18	10.152	
Gross present value			78.372	(B)
less Capital outlay			54.000	(A)
Net present value (B-A)			**+24.372**	

The annual net cash flows shown in column 2 are multiplied by the 10% discount factors in column 1 to produce the annual present value of the cash flows in column 3. These annual present values are then added together to give the gross present value of the net cash inflows of £78.372 million. Alternatively, you may have realised that the same result would be achieved from multiplying the net cash inflows by the sum of the discount factors, that is £18m x (0.909 + 0.826 + 0.751 + 0.683 + 0.621 + 0.564). A constant sum of money like this £18m is known in financial terms as an annuity. (Annuity tables are readily available to prevent the necessity of summing the discount factors.)

The net present value for Proposal 1 is calculated by deducting the capital outlay from the gross present values of the net cash inflows (i.e. £78.372 million - £54 million) giving £24.372 million. The same type of calculation for Proposals 2 and 3 produces the following values which are summarised alongside those for Proposal 1 in *Table 4.3.*

Table 4.3   *N.P.V's*

	Proposal 1 £m	Proposal 2 £m	Proposal 3 £m
Gross present value	78.372	65.261	82.093
less Capital outlay	54	45	65
Net present value	**+ 24.372**	**+ 20.261**	**+17.093**

The results show that for all three proposals the net present value is positive, and on economic grounds are acceptable because they:

O   exceed the required rate of return of 10%;

O   cover the capital outlay and,

O   produce a sum in excess of the capital outlay which is referred to as the net present value.

Internal Rate of Return (IRR)

As illustrated in *Figure 4.4*, the IRR is the rate which equates the gross present value with the capital outlay associated with the investment opportunity. At the IRR the NPV is zero.

Figure 4.4   IRR,   Gross present value equals capital outlay

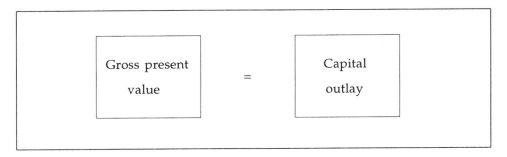

In terms of a decision, if the IRR exceeds the rate of return required by investors (the cost of capital) then, in principle, the opportunity is economically viable and vice versa if it is not.

An advantage of this approach is that it is not necessary to know the cost of capital in order to undertake the calculation. This is arguably quite useful in a divisional setting when it may not be in the interest of the organisation as a whole to publicise the exact percentage return that is to be achieved. It is also reckoned that it is simpler for managers to work with a percentage - it is easier to say: The rate of return on the project is X%, rather than, the project has a positive net present value when discounted at Y% (the companys' required rate of return). However, there are some shortcomings associated with the approach that we will consider later.

IRR illustration

Remember that whereas the calculation of the net present value is reliant upon the company's cost of capital as data input, the IRR is not.

Let us review the IRR using Proposal 1. At 10% it produces a large NPV. Given that the IRR corresponds with an NPV of £0, the discount factor must be increased significantly in order to achieve the scaling down of the NPV required. Following the same procedure for calculating the NPV as earlier but using a 20% discount factor the result is £5.85m. Clearly a higher rate is required, so let us try 25%. This results in a negative NPV of £0.864m. The IRR must fall somewhere in between and is 24.3%.

Similar calculations for Proposals 2 and 3 produce the following results which are shown alongside that calculated earlier for Proposal 1:

	Proposal 1	**Proposal 2**	**Proposal 3**
Internal rate of return %	24.3	27.5	23.1

The internal rate of return does have to be used somewhat guardedly. Whereas the net present value decision rule assumes that cash flows resulting during the life cycle of a proposal have an opportunity cost equal to the discount rate used, the internal rate of return decision rule assumes that such resulting cash flows have an opportunity cost equal to the internal rate of return which generated them.

The net present value approach provides an absolute measure of the increase in value of the company if a particular proposal is undertaken. By comparison the internal rate of return provides a percentage figure, however, the value cannot be seen. This can be appreciated if we compare Proposals 1 and 2. The box around the NPV and IRR figures in Table 4.4 highlights that Proposal 1 with the higher NPV has a lower IRR. Given no limit on funding and faced with a choice between either Proposal 1 or Proposal 2, selecting that with the highest IRR would result in less value being created.

Table 4.4   NPV or IRR?

	Proposal 1 £m	Proposal 2 £m	Proposal 3 £m
Net present value	+ 24.372	+ 20.261	+17.093
Internal rate of return%	24.3	27.5	23.14

It is important to recognise that Proposals 1 and 2 involve different capital outlays. In such circumstances the gross present value can be divided by the capital outlay to determine which produces the best value per £1 of outlay.

As we have indicated, the maximisation of shareholder wealth is the commonly accepted objective for commercial organisations and this can be most appropriately gauged using the net present value approach.

At this point it is appropriate to place our discussion within the context of financial theory reviewed in *Chapter 1*. There you may recall we made reference to the "Present Value Rule" (*Fisher-Hirshleifer Model*) which provided proof many years ago why in a world of certainty accepting all projects with a positive NPV maximises the wealth of shareholders.

Inflation

Short-term interest rates in percentage terms per annum in February 1994 ranged from 3.38% for Singapore to 10,723% for Brazil. The majority of the others were closer to the lower of the two, with only Russia approaching anything like Brazil with a rate of 593%. Why the differences? Well, there are many reasons, but one important distinguishing characteristic of these economies is the effect of inflation - Russia and Brazil are suffering the effects of hyper-inflation (excessive inflation).

In fact, in all types of economies inflation has to be dealt with and must never be ignored. It may be obvious for hyper-inflation economies, but what about others like the UK? Does it really matter? The answer is yes! That it does was demonstrated by *Dimson and Marsh* of The London Business School who found from their contacts with large British companies that many have not responded sufficiently to falling inflation (and lower interest) rates. The consequence of this is that profitable investments may well be turned away, or an excessive return may well be demanded from those which are accepted [1].

So far we have ignored inflation, but you clearly cannot in real life. For example, in the UK, rates of inflation have approached 15% even in the last ten years, although it is fair to say that inflation has been much lower in the years of the recession of the early 1990's. The problem is that even adding 2 or 3% to the cash flows because of likely inflation will add about 2 or 3% to the rate of return that should be expected from the project.

So, how do you deal with inflation? The answer is by making specific adjustments if necessary. So, if in evaluating potential opportunities the discount rate to be used includes some allowance for inflation, the cash flows to be discounted should also include some allowance for inflation. Otherwise one would not be comparing like with like.

The evaluation of any investment opportunity requires good financial judgement to be exercised about a future which is uncertain. Thus, if prices are expected to change because of inflation, then this must be incorporated within any appraisal.

Unfortunately, many managers make the mistake of believing that by adopting discounted cash flow techniques, inflation has automatically been incorporated into the financial appraisal. Nothing could be further from the truth because as you may recall, the principle of discounting is derived from the principle of compound interest. Even in a world with no inflation some compound interest would be present, insofar as the providers of finance would require some compensation for foregoing their wealth for a period of time. This being so the principle of discounting would be equally applicable. The omission of inflation from an evaluation can change views as to the economic viability of a proposal as we will illustrate with reference to the net present value calculation for Proposal 1.

Let us assume that the 10% discount factor used excluded any allowance for inflation, but that inflation has been built into the cash flows. The position now is that the rate which should have been used to take account of inflation is 21%. How is this arrived at? Well, let us assume that the estimate of average inflation for the 6 year period which has been built into the cash flows is 10%. Given a required rate of return without inflation (known as a *real* rate, r) of 10% and the estimate for inflation (i) of 10%, the required rate of return with inflation (known as the *money* or *nominal* rate, m) can be calculated using the following formula:

$$(1 + m) \qquad = \qquad (1+r) \ (1+i)$$

$$1.21, \text{ or } 21\% \qquad = \qquad (1.10) \ (1.10)$$

In *Table 4.5* we illustrate the effect upon the economic viability of Proposal 1 when it is discounted at 21%:

Table 4.5   Discounting Proposal 1 at 21%

	Column 1	Column 2	Column 3 (Col. 1 x Col. 2)
	Discounted cash flow factor	Cash flows	Present value
Year	21%	£m	£m
1	0.826	18	14.868
2	0.683	18	12.294
3	0.564	18	10.152
4	0.467	18	8.406
5	0.386	18	6.948
6	0.319	18	5.742
Gross present value			58.410 (B)
less Capital outlay			54.000 (A)
Net present value (B-A)			+4.410
Net present value at 10%			+24.372

The fall of nearly £20m in NPV from discounting at 21% rather than 10% shows that there can be quite a difference in results if inflation is taken into account.

Table 4.6   Discounting deflated cash flows for Proposal 1

	Deflation factor	Cash flows	Deflated cash flows	Discounted cash flow factor	Present value
Year	10%	£m	£m	10%	£m
1	0.909	18	16.362	0.909	14.873
2	0.826	18	14.868	0.826	12.281
3	0.751	18	13.518	0.751	10.152
4	0.683	18	12.294	0.683	8.397
5	0.621	18	11.178	0.621	6.942
6	0.564	18	10.152	0.564	5.726
Gross present value					58.371 (B)
less Capital outlay					54.000 (A)
Net present value (B-A)					+ 4.371

In the case of Proposal 1 we dealt with inflation by increasing the discount rate. However, we could also have decreased the cash flows by removing the effect of inflation from them and then by discounting the result by the required rate of return excluding inflation. In terms of Proposal 1 this would involve discounting the cash flows at 10% to remove the effect of inflation and then discounting the resulting cash flows at the 10% required rate of return as shown in the *Table 4.6*.

There is a difference in the NPV results shown in the two tables, this being attributable to rounding differences associated with the discount and deflation factors. When cash flows in Tables 4.5 and 4.6 are discounted using DCF factors calculated to six decimal places, the gross present value is 58.503 in both cases. To summarise, inflation should be dealt with in either of two ways:

- ◯ The cash flows generated by a project can be forecast in nominal terms, that is where an estimate for inflation affecting the cash flows is taken into account, and then the subsequent cash flows are discounted at a nominal rate.

- ◯ Alternatively, the cash flows expected from the project can be estimated in constant or real prices, that is today's prices, without taking into account any expected inflation rates, and then discounted at a real rate.

We believe that the most important issue to understand is how inflation is likely to effect the cash flows from a project. If inflation affects all prices generally the same, then the real and the nominal approaches will provide the same answer. However, it is often the case that individual cash flow elements in the appraisal, such as the sales revenue, labour costs, materials cost and the like, may not all be subject to the same degree of inflation, or price variation. In such circumstances, where there are different rates, then an adjustment should be made to each.

In general we believe that the most accurate and, therefore, the best approach is to deal with cash flows in nominal terms.   However, there are cases where it is sometimes better to think in real terms by excluding any consideration of inflation in the cash flows, and then discounting at a real rate. For example, in countries with hyper-inflation such as in Brazil and Russia where the rates of inflation are currently very high, excluding any consideration of inflation in cash flows would be advantageous because

- ◯ it is very difficult to estimate what exactly the rate of inflation will be and certainly it is difficult to establish a nominal discount rate over a period of very high inflation, and

- ◯ the numbers often become very large in the computations such that calculators cannot handle them.

In such hyper-inflation situation it may not be necessary to adjust the discount rate from a nominal to a real value. How is this achieved? For example, if the nominal rate is 1,340% and the inflation rate is 1,100% we can convert to a real rate using the formula we outlined earlier, i.e.

$$(1 + m) \quad = \quad (1 + r) \ (1 + i)$$

$$\text{Therefore,} \quad (1 + r) \quad = \quad (1 + m) \div (1 + i)$$

And given the earlier numbers the real rate is:

$$1.20, \text{ or } 20\% = \quad (1 + 13.4) \div (1 + 11.0), \text{ i.e. } (14.4) \div (12.0)$$

To summarise, inflation has to be dealt with in its own right and must never be ignored.

Dealing with taxation

One other area which will impact upon a cash flow to be used in evaluating an investment opportunity concerns taxation. The specifics of taxation are complex and well beyond the scope of this book, however, the general principle to follow is similar to that discussed with regard to inflation. Just as in discounting cash flows to calculate a project's net present value where inflated cash flows must be discounted using an interest rate which contains an allowance for inflation, so too must the cash flows discounted be either before or after tax, depending upon whether the required discount rate is a before or after tax rate.

Throughout this book we will follow the approach of discounting after tax cash flows at an after tax required rate of return. Building the effects of taxation into the cash flows is relatively straight forward in principle, as we will demonstrate in the next chapter. How to estimate an after tax required rate of return we will consider in *Chapter 7* when we review the whole subject of the required rate of return (often called the cost of capital).

The importance of good quality data

In evaluating any potential opportunity of the type we have been considering, great care must be taken to ensure that the quality of input data is as good as possible. There are two important issues concerning such data:

○ How are initial cash flow estimates to be generated as accurately as possible?

○ How can the importance of the various components within the estimate be judged?

With regard to the first of these, various forecasting methods are available to help in the generation of estimates. Quite how initial estimates can be generated we will discuss in some detail in the next chapter. However, what is important to appreciate now is that initial estimates should be broken down as far as possible. To use information about net annual cash flows alone is unsatisfactory and it should be broken down further. This is because a breakdown into key factors can be combined with the use of a computer spreadsheet package to investigate the importance of each factor to the end result.

Just exactly what factors should be used in cash flow estimation? The following list includes the kind of data that may need to be considered:

○ Sales forecast

○ Product life

○ Discount policy

○ Promotional costs

○ Selling costs

○ Market test costs

○ Competitive advantages and disadvantages

○ Transportation costs

○ Operating costs

○ Material and supply costs

○ Start-up costs

○ Shut-down costs

○ Maintenance costs

○ Repair costs

○ Capacity utilisation and new capital expenditure

○ Inflation

○ Risk

○ Taxation

○ Residual value

○ Working capital

○ Competitors' reactions

From this list there are three issues in particular upon which we will focus attention. These are areas of critical importance that are all too often overlooked relative to other issues:

○ Risk

○ Residual value

○ Competitors reactions

The first of these, risk, is absolutely crucial to take into consideration and, as you will see from this and subsequent chapters, in a number of different ways. Residual value and competitors' reactions are, from our experience, two areas that can be grossly overlooked and are particularly important in appraising opportunities with strategic implications.

Risk and uncertainty

Any investment opportunity with long-term implications must, by definition be subject to some risk or uncertainty. Somehow this risk must be captured in any economic valuation and it should come as no surprise to find that there is more than one way of achieving this. Here, we will consider the most popular approach we have encountered which is known as *sensitivity analysis* [2]. With this approach the assumptions surrounding a project can be input to computer software to produce a base case typically focusing upon the internal rate of return. From this, changes in assumption can easily be made to gauge the effect upon its internal rate of return. The mechanics of such an application we will now consider using the following data relating to Proposal 1, discussed earlier:

Capital costs
a. Initial expenditure £54 million
b. Life 6 years
c. Scrap (residual value), nil

Annual revenues
a. Sales volume 600,000 units
b. Selling price £50 per unit

Annual costs
a. Labour £5 per unit
b. Materials £15 per unit

In practice, the data would have to be far more detailed, but we have deliberately made the example as simple as possible to facilitate exposition of the approach and the advantages of such an application.

You will recall that we calculated NPV and IRR values earlier in this chapter using this data. We have recalculated these values to remove the rounding effect present in earlier calculations to produce a net present value of £24.372m using a discount rate of 10%, a net present value of £4.41m using a discount rate of 21%, and an internal rate of return of 24.3%. Without the need to input any more data each of the input variables - capital outlay, the time horizon or life, sales volume and price, labour cost, and materials cost - can be varied by a specific percentage to demonstrate the effect of such a change upon the NPV and IRR. This is illustrated in the following *Tables 4.7 and 4.8* where each of these input variables have been varied adversely by 10% and the NPVs and IRR recalculated.

Table 4.7   An eye to the "downside"

	Original estimate	Varied adversely by 10%
Capital outlay	£54 million	£59.4 million
Life	6	5.4
Sales volume	600,000	540,000
Selling price	£50	£45
Labour cost	£5	£5.5
Materials	£15	£16.5

Table 4.8   Downside effect on NPV and IRR

	NPV at 10%	NPV at 21%	IRR
Capital outlay	£18.97m	£-0.99m	20.3%
Life	£18.30m	£0.96m	21.8%
Sales volume	£16.54m	£-1.43m	19.9%
Selling price	£11.31m	£-5.33m	16.9%
Labour cost	£23.07m	£3.44m	23.6%
Materials cost	£20.45m	£1.49m	22.1%

In the case of Proposal 1 we can see from *Table 4.8* that if the 21% discount factor is appropriate the potential prospects of a 10% change in individual input variables look bleak to say the least. The worst result arises from a 10% decrease in the selling price. According to this scenario the result is a negative NPV of £5.33m and an IRR of more than four percentage points below the required rate of return. At this rate only changes in the life, labour cost and materials cost result in a positive NPV. By comparison, such a 10% adverse change to these input variables assuming a 10% discount factor results in a positive NPV in all cases.

What such analysis clearly points to is the need to review the input data used in generating the cash flows very closely. An analysis of the market and competitive forces, together with the relationship between key variables would clearly be warranted. For example, if the price is decreased by how much, if at all, would the volume sold increase.

Considerable attention also needs to be paid to determining the required rate of return as accurately as possible. As we have seen, the view of Proposal 1 changes drastically between 10% and 21% and, as you will see, valuation can be affected significantly by small changes in the discount rate. So what really should this rate be? This is a very important issue and one we look at closely in *Chapter 7.*

In practice, the analysis would be extended much further than in the example so as to explore changes in a number of variables and any interrelationships between variables, such as price and volume sold. Nevertheless, what this example serves to illustrate is how potential uncertainty can be readily built into an evaluation of a potential opportunity.

Residual value

One element that should never be overlooked concerns the residual value of a potential investment opportunity. Typically in applying DCF techniques the assumption made is that any residual value at the end of the life of a project corresponds with the liquidation value of any fixed and current assets in the final year. In other words, if there is any such residual it corresponds with a release of cash which is then discounted back to a present value together with all other cash flows.

As you will see in *Chapter 6* this is too simplistic when looking at the value derived from a strategic investment opportunity. In such cases, determining the relevant time horizon over which to discount may itself be fraught with problems. Second, even if this can be estimated satisfactorily, there is a good reason for not assuming that everything terminates at the end of the horizon selected. It may well be the case that value will continue to be created, in which case we need to be able to measure it.

What about competitors' reactions?

It is all too easy in evaluating investment opportunities to consider only the detailed numerical input about sales and cost of sales which are then checked line for line over an estimated lifetime for internal consistency without any attempt at modelling the potential effect upon the cash flows as a result competitors' reactions. It needs to be recognised that scenarios for competitors' reactions can usually be generated by harnessing internal managerial knowledge and experience and by a thorough external appraisal.

Why is the analysis of competitors' reactions so important? The first entrants with new products have a head start on the competition and may have some longer-term competitive advantage, for example, in terms of product protection via trade marks. But, the successful introduction of a new product will attract competing products and competition will tend to force prices down.

Cash flow projections undertaken should recognise market developments and likely competitors' reactions. How this can be achieved we will review in the next two chapters and is strongly linked with the residual value issue.

Concluding remarks

We have now reviewed the financial techniques that can be used to evaluate a potential strategic investment opportunity and important issues associated with their application. However, we have left a number of questions unanswered as yet, like - how can cash flows be generated using knowledge of the business environment? How can any long-term value be measured? And, how should competitors' reactions and other important strategic issues be dealt with? It is to these issues we turn in the next three chapters.

Appendix - Non DCF Evaluation Techniques

Payback period

The payback period measures how long it will take to recover the capital outlay from cash inflows. It is calculated using cash flow data and is expressed in terms of a number of years, or years and months. For Proposal 1 which has a capital outlay of £54 million and cash inflows of £18 million for each year of its expected life of 6 years, the payback is clearly 3 years (3 years x £18 million = capital outlay of £54 million).

If you try to calculate the payback period for the other two proposals you will find that it does not occur exactly at the end of a year. For example, Proposal 2 generates the following cash inflows:

	Net annual cash inflows £m	Accumulated annual cash £m
Year 1	21	21
Year 2	18	39
Year 3	12	51

The cash flows for the first two years amount to £39 million. In the third year, only £6 million of the net cash flows are required to make the accumulated net cash flows equal to the £45 million capital outlay. By assuming that the cash inflows occur evenly throughout the year we can find the payback period in years and months. The years we have established as being two and the number of months can be found by expressing the cash inflows during year 3 required to payback as a fraction of the total cash inflows during year three, and then converting the result to months as follows:

$$\frac{\text{Cash flow required to payback}}{\text{Cash inflow during payback year}} \quad x \quad 12 \text{ months}$$

$$\frac{£6m}{£12m} \quad x \quad 12 \text{ months}$$

$$= \quad 6 \text{ months}$$

The same calculation for Proposal 3 produces a payback period of 2 years 2 months and the results for all three proposals may be summarised as:

	Proposal 1	Proposal 2	Proposal 3
Payback period	3 years exactly	2 years 6 months	2 years 2 months

A simple ranking, in this case based on the proposal offering the shortest payback period, shows that Proposal 3 is the most desirable.

The payback period has a distinct advantage over other methods because it is relatively simple to calculate, understand and implement. Against this the payback period focuses specifically upon the time taken to recover the capital outlay such that cash flows generated after the payback period may be easily overlooked. One other major shortcoming is that unless the cash flows are specifically adjusted, the time value of money is ignored.

Accounting rate of return

The accounting rate of return can be likened to the profit on assets (return on capital employed) ratio, insofar as the return generated by a proposal is expressed as a percentage of the investment outlay. Unlike the payback period the data used in its calculation includes that relating to its whole life. You must be aware, however, that it is calculated with reference to a proposal's profit rather than cash flow and it is sometimes criticised because it can be calculated in a number of different ways. Indeed different users may arrive at different rates of return using the same input data, and what is even more confusing is that none of the resulting calculations are necessarily incorrect!

The first step in calculating the accounting rate of return is to accumulate the estimated annual profit flows to establish the total profit of the proposal. If only cash flow information is available then the annual cash flows must be summed, from which the capital outlay must be deducted to give the total profit. The total profit is required in order to calculate the average annual profit. This is found by dividing the profit by the estimated life of the proposals and is illustrated for our three example proposals in the following table:

		Proposal 1 £m	Proposal 2 £m	Proposal 3 £m
Total cash inflow		108	85	101
Outlay		54	45	65
Total profit	(a)	54	40	36
Life (years)	(b)	6	5	4
Average annual profit	(a)÷(b)	£9m	£8m	£9m

The rate of return is then calculated by dividing the average annual profit by the outlay. For Proposal 1 the calculation is:

$$\text{Accounting rate of return (\%)} = \frac{\text{Average annual profit}}{\text{Outlay}} \times 100$$

$$= \frac{\text{£9 m}}{\text{£54m}} \times 100$$

$$= 16.7\%$$

Similar calculations for Proposals 2 and 3 produce accounting rates of return of 17.8% and 13.9% respectively. A simple ranking, which in this case is based on the highest accounting rate of return, shows that Proposal 2 is slightly better than Proposal 1.

	Proposal 1	Proposal 2	Proposal 3
Accounting rate of return %	16.7	17.8	13.8
Ranking	2	1	3

It was indicated earlier that using the same input data, different accounting rates of return can be produced. How can this happen? Some organisations use the average rather than the total capital outlay. As you will appreciate, anything that reduces the outlay in the calculation will increase the rate of return. The potential ambiguity in accounting rate of return results is sometimes presented as being a theoretical shortcoming. Nevertheless, the technique is popular in some organisations, particularly where manuals of capital expenditure procedure provide a specific definition of the items to be used in rate of return calculations.

References

1.   Dimson E. and Marsh P., "Unhappy Returns", Financial Times, Wednesday February 9, 1994, p17.

2.   For example, see Euro Disneyland S.C.A., Offer for Sale, S.G. Warburg Securities, 1989

5

Estimating Free Cash Flows

"Garbage In, Garbage Out"

- *Anon.*

Introduction

We have shown how to use discounted cash flow analysis in evaluating a strategic investment opportunity and the importance of data estimates in determining its desirability in economic terms, but this begs a key question - how do you estimate sound cash flows? Insights into the evaluation of large capital projects in practice has revealed that there may often be a major problem in generating appropriate and relevant input data. In fact, the quality of the output is heavily dependent upon the input, a point captured by the expression *GIGO - Garbage In Garbage Out.* So are there any important characteristics of relevant data?

Relevant data

It must be *future oriented* - that is it must be *yet to be incurred*. Data about the past is irrelevant, apart from its use in forecasting. For example, a past or "sunk" cost cannot be affected by a decision relating to the future. It should, therefore, be ignored. The only costs that will be affected by a decision are those which are actually incremental to that decision, that is, those incurred as a consequence of taking the decision.

There are many occasions when the appropriate cost or value of an item will not be found in the accounting records. For example, in a decision about what to do with a piece of land owned by a business we can think of there being three pieces of financial information. First, there is the historical cost of the land as shown in the business' accounts. Second, there is the resale value, and third there is the value to the business from using the land for purposes of expansion. The historical cost is not relevant because it is a sunk, or past cost. The only data that is relevant are the other two values and any decision will have to be based partially on figures which are not included in the results or budgets of the business. It will only be worthwhile using the land for expanding the business if the additional benefit from the expansion is greater than the loss of rent that would be receivable from leasing the land, or the cash that would be generated from its sale.

So can historical information be of any value at all? Certainly it can be used as a starting point for making estimates about the future and, as you will see later in this chapter, this is just the approach we initially apply to the information about *Meunier plc* we introduced in *Chapter 2*. One good practical illustration of how past information may be used effectively can be seen if we consider *Euro Disney*.

As has been revealed widely in the press, *Euro Disney* has faced some very difficult times. Despite these, however, other parties have shown considerable interest in theme parks and are keen to learn from relevant past experience. One very interested party is *Grand Peninsula*, which owns the theme park site called Tibigardens outside Salou, near Tarragona, on Spain's Mediterranean coast [1].

Tibigardens is a Pta41bn (£200m) theme park which is very close to completion. Comparisons are difficult with *Euro Disney* because of the different scale of the two projects. Whilst Paris attracts 11m visitors a year, Tibigardens expects 2.7 million in its first year and, despite being the second largest European park, its highest ambitions are well short of *Euro Disney's*. Hopes are for its attendance to rise to 3.5 million and eventually 5 million.

The differences between Tibigardens and *Euro Disney* are:

○   Tibigardens is just a theme park and has avoided high fixed costs by shelving plans to build a large beach side hotel and 2,000 living units. Arguably *Euro Disney* got its theme park right and what went wrong was its inability to fill six hotels. Because Tibigardens is in a resort area, including Benidorm, it does not need to build hotels. There are some 800,000 hotel beds within 200km. The park is aimed at holidaymakers who will visit the attractions for a day trip.

○   Tibigardens will only open for 156 days a year between April and October, unlike Euro Disneyland which is open all year round. The climate in Spain is consistently warmer and sunnier and during these 156 days more than 15 million foreign tourists are normally in striking distance of the park.

○   The financial structure of the two parks differs. One estimate put total fees in royalties and management payable by *Euro Disney* to *Walt Disney* at 31.5% of operating income when the Paris park opened in 1992, and are supposed to rise. For Tibigardens fees payable will fall from 12.4% of operating income when the park opens in 1995 to 10.4% in 1998 and should decrease further.

The Tibigardens project is expected to be profitable because of drawing upon the hindsight mistakes of *Euro Disney*.   In fact, for Tibigardens it is reckoned that the profitable components of Euro Disney have simply been put together.

It is important to recognise that risks are much easier to assess when there is relevant experience to draw upon because more realistic scenarios are easier to develop. Whilst arguably with hindsight the *Euro Disney* shortcomings should have been seen, it is reasonable to argue that experience was limited. (In fact, the old saying "a genius is a fool who succeeds" may probably be appropriate to reflect upon at this point!)

Cash flow "drivers"

In the last chapter we were conveniently provided with cash flow information for all three proposals, but how were they determined? In this section we will demonstrate how the future cash flows expected to be generated by a strategic investment opportunity can be estimated. In very simple terms you will see that it involves estimating potential growth in sales and the margin to be made on those sales from which it is possible to form a view of likely cash inflows. Having estimated cash inflows, associated cash outflows will have to be taken into consideration. For example, taxation will have to be taken into account and also the amount of capital that needs to be invested to support current and future sales.

In fact, to generate a free cash flow forecast we can use the first five of the seven value drivers outlined in the last section of *Chapter 3* with reference to Shareholder Value Analysis. These five we will refer to as cash flow drivers, and are as follows:

1. Sales growth rate

2. Operating profit margin

3. Cash tax rate

4. Fixed capital investment

5. Working capital investment

Given these five cash flow drivers, how do we establish values for them in any particular case? Quite simply, they may be estimated by looking at a mix of past experience, management judgement about what is likely to happen in the future, and observations about the marketplace.

As we indicated earlier, it is vital not to underestimate the importance of the cash flow data in measuring business value. We have already referred to Garbage In, Garbage Out (GIGO) which is very apt for issues relating to business valuation - the quality of any business valuation can only be as good as the input data upon which it is based. With this in mind let us review the issues associated with estimating the cash flow drivers.

Sales growth forecasts

Estimated future sales can be projected from market information to produce forecasts about the markets for products or services, market shares and the potential for pricing policy. Such market forecasts should be based upon an analysis of market opportunities and the development of product strategies to supply those markets discovered from such analysis. Each product group will have to forecast a level of sales applicable to each market sector. A pricing policy will also have to be established in each sector in order to put a monetary value on the forecast sales quantities. Obviously, prices (in most markets) affect the quantity sold, so there will be an interactive process to establish an expected level of sales quantity at the most appropriate prices to provide what is thought to be the optimal level of planned sales value.

As we have illustrated, the level of current sales (for each product at current prices) will be the starting point. To that will be added expected growth in sales value which will come either from increased volumes of sales or increased prices. There may also be some decreases from anticipated decline in volumes, and even some lowering of prices. To the current level of sales will have to be added the additional growth in sales which will come from investment policies into new products, new markets, etc.

It is quite logical to think of the first driver of business value as being sales growth. If the enterprise does not sell anything, then it cannot really be said to be in business! In a sense, this also goes for non-for-profit organisations. Perhaps one does not think of their activities as "sales" but the level of activity they expect to be involved in or level of service they expect to provide, sets the scene for the facilities required to support that level of performance.

Operating profit margin

Once sales forecasts and more concrete sales plans are agreed, managers will need to consider the means of ensuring the supply of those sales to customers, and the costs of doing so. Such costs will relate to:

○ sourcing raw materials and estimating the costs of raw materials

○ employment and training of an adequate labour force

○ establishment of sufficient sales and distribution facilities

○ ensuring production facilities are adequate

○ creating a management team able to manage the business

In a not-for-profit organisation activities will also generate costs that have to be charged against sales. However, in some not-for-profit concerns the income may not be linked to the service in quite the same way that costs are linked to sales in a commercial enterprise, such as a charity where the income is from donations and grants unrelated to the "output" or activity of the charity. In this case, the not-for-profit undertaking has to ensure that the best use is made of the income it has by providing as cost effective a service as is possible. It is arguably more difficult to manage this - where one is measuring benefits against costs - than in the commercial world where the amount of profit is a measure of the degree of success.

What this illustration also flags up is that very different approaches may need to be adopted in generating forecast cash flows depending upon circumstances. What drives cash flow is by no mean common to all types of business operations, an issue that has to be considered in forecasting future cash flows. The sequence of events that we have described starting with sales growth may be difficult to apply in all circumstances.

It is important to realise that the profit margin on sales depends on the type of business one is in. Generally, the principle is that the greater the need for investment in fixed assets and working capital, the higher the profit margin has to be on sales. For example, food retailers in the UK have relatively low amounts tied up in fixed assets and working capital - they may own some of their stores, but also rent others, and have very little tied up in working capital - low stocks and probably no debtors. Such companies work on a sales margin of 5-6%. By comparison, heavy goods companies like those supplying plant and equipment to industry, have to plan for much higher margins on sales value. Such companies have large factories to pay for and the net profit on each sale has proportionately to be much higher than the retailer - something in the order of 12-15% or more.

Cash tax flows

Once operating profit has been estimated, a forecast amount of tax to be paid on those profits will have to be taken into account. However, tax is more difficult to consider from a general managerial perspective than the other cash flow drivers because it is very much a specialist area. For this reason you may often find general assumptions about the cash tax rate being used in running a business. Nevertheless, there are one or two issues that are important for you to understand.

Tax payable upon profits is an income tax paid by a venture on its income (or net profit) in just the same way that individuals have to pay income tax on their income. Companies in many countries must also pay capital gains tax on any gain made from holding an asset or investment over time. Thus, if an office building were sold for £10m which had originally cost £4m, there would be tax to pay on the capital appreciation of £6m. Actually, in many countries though the capital gains tax is not levied on the full capital gain - an allowance is made for the general rate of inflation. In this example, the £4m original cost would be indexed to a higher figure and the resultant gain would be lower. Furthermore, companies actually accrue capital gains tax, as time goes by. So a charge, for what has become known as deferred tax, is made in each year's accounts for the amount of capital gains tax that would have to be paid if the asset were sold at the date the accounts were drawn up.

The point about deferred tax is that it is irrelevant as far as free cash flow is concerned. Our concern is with the amount of tax actually payable and, more particularly, when, that is the year during which it is payable. Tax on the net profits - or corporation tax as it is known in the UK - is payable after the end of the year to which the profits relate. This is because it is not possible until after the end of the year to calculate the actual net profit on which the tax is calculated! The tax on capital gains is not payable, however, until an asset is sold and the gain realised, thus the date of payment of the tax may be many years hence. Thus, although the deferred tax calculated on the basis of the potential capital gain is charged against profit over the years, the tax is not paid until the asset is sold. The tax payment date, however, is important when budgeting for free cash flow many years ahead.

Operating cash flow

What we have discussed above with reference to sales forecasts, operating profit margin and tax cash flows enables operating profit to be estimated. However, it is important to recognise the potential complexity that may be involved in deriving operating profit in reality. First, many businesses produce multiple products and/or provide multiple services, meaning that the future overall operating profit may be most meaningfully and accurately calculated by undertaking a number of computations which are then aggregated to form a total view. Second, in so doing, constraints upon the business have to be recognised. These constraints are often referred to as "limiting factors" in accounting/finance. Basically, one has to recognise that, for example, the market conditions may constrain the potential sales growth and/or the operating profit margin. One such factor will often predominate and has to be taken into consideration in ensuring realism in developing forecasts.

It is vital not to lose sight of the fact that operating profit may often not be the same as operating cash flow. Accounting attempts to report a "true and fair" view of the affairs of a business, and there are several accruals and apportionments which have to be made which often make operating profit very different from operating cash flow. A major difference between the two is because of the apportionment against "cash income" for depreciation of assets.

Depreciation can be thought of as being an apportionment of the sum paid for a fixed asset over its useful economic life. The simplest way to understand this is with reference to an illustration. Imagine a piece of machinery bought today for £100,000, which is expected to last for 5 years, and to be worth nothing at the end of this time period. If paid for by cash then there would be a cash outflow of £100,000 at the time of purchase. However, for accounting purposes it would be written off over the 5 year period, such that only a proportion, say one fifth or £20,000, would be charged against profit each year.

Operating cash flow will typically be considerably more than operating profit. This point is well illustrated in the cash flow statements UK and US companies are required to produce in addition to a profit and loss account and balance sheet. In *Table 5.1* we illustrate the difference between operating cash flow and operating profit by way of a note provided to the cash flow statement in the 1992 report and accounts for the *BP (British Petroleum) Group plc* [2]:

Table 5.1 Group cash flow statement

Reconciliation of historical cost profit before interest and tax to net cash inflow from operating activities

	1992 £m	1993 £m
Profit Before Interest and Tax (historical cost)	784	1,926
Depreciation	2,390	2,079
Exploration expenditure written off	364	425
Share of profits of associated undertakings, dividends and interest receivable	-389	-454
Charge for provisions	151	222
Profit on disposals	-70	-242
Decrease in stocks	30	585
Decrease in debtors	223	244
Increase (decrease) in creditors	11	-545
Net cash inflow from operating activities	3,494	4,240

Depreciation and other similar items are shown to be added back in *Table 5.1* and other items like stocks, debtors and creditors are taken into consideration to arrive at the entry for "Net cash flow from operating activities". Furthermore, a direct link with the profit and loss account is shown in this note, for which the first entry is "Historical cost profit before interest and tax" taken from the Group's profit and loss account.

Fixed and working capital investment

The distinction between operating cash flow and free cash flow is that investment necessary to support the future cash flows is taken into consideration in deriving free cash flow. Such investment will concerned with:

1. Replacement Fixed Capital Investment (RFCI), that is investment in replacement fixed assets to maintain the level of productive facilities currently in place.

2. Incremental Fixed Capital Investment (IFCI), that is investment in new assets to provide additional facilities to enable intended sales growth to occur.

3. Incremental Working Capital Investment (IWCI), that is investment in additional working capital, such as stocks of materials.

All of these three have to be estimated which can be difficult in practice, and for which many different approaches can be adopted. As regards the first, replacement capital expenditure, a frequent assumption is that depreciation is a good estimate, the implications being that what is added back to operating profit by way of depreciation to calculate operating cash flow, will be deducted from operating cash flow to derive free cash flow. For the other two investments, which represent additional or incremental expenditure necessary to support the intended sales growth, there are many different forecasting approaches that can be used. A popular approach that we illustrated earlier is to estimate the relationship between increased sales and increased fixed and working capital expenditure using historical data.

Producing a free cash flow estimate

To see how they can be used to provide a free cash flow estimate, let us consider the following example:

Assume a business with sales revenue today of £100m and sales growth rate expectations of 5% in the first year, 10% in the second and third years, and 15% for the remaining years. With knowledge of this information the sales receipts would be as indicated by the figures in italics in *Table 5.2*.

Table 5.2   Forecasting future sales revenue

Now	Year 1	Year 2	Year 3	Year 4	Year 5	Year 6
£100m						
x 1.05 =	£105m					
	x 1.10 =	£115.5m				
		x 1.10 =	£127.05m			
			x 1.15 =	£146.11m		
				x 1.15 =	£168.03m	
					x 1.15 =	£193.23m
£100m	£105m	£115.5m	£127.05m	£146.11m	£168.03m	£193.23m

The values of the operating profit margin and the cash tax rate for these years have been estimated as follows:

Operating profit margin	10%	10%	12%	12%	14%	10%
Cash tax rate	30%	30%	30%	30%	30%	30%

Applying these two to the cash flows calculated earlier, results in the after tax operating profit shown in *Table 5.3*.

Table 5.3   *From sales receipts to after tax operating profit*

Year	1	2	3	4	5	6
	£m	£m	£m	£m	£m	£m
Sales receipts	105.00	115.50	127.05	146.11	168.03	193.23
Operating profit margin	x10%	x10%	x12%	x12%	x14%	x10%
Operating profit	10.50	11.55	15.25	17.53	23.52	19.32
Cash tax rate	-30%	-30%	-30%	-30%	-30%	-30%
After tax operating profit	7.35	8.09	10.68	12.27	16.46	13.52

What is required is cash flow and not profit. As we indicated earlier, the main difference between the two is because of the apportionment against "cash income" for depreciation of assets. In addition, the normal process of accounting adopted by businesses, known as *accrual accounting*, means that there will be other deductions from income, known as provisions (for anticipated costs which have not yet come to fruition), such as provisions for possible bad debts. To be prudent (conservative) businesses make a provision for bad debts against current income based upon past experience. This will further depress accounting profit but not necessarily actual cash earned because the basis for the provision is only an expectation.

For our example company, let us assume that the depreciation for each of the six years has been estimated as £5m. This means that the after tax operating cash flow is £5m higher than the operating profit for each year:

Year	1	2	3	4	5	6
	£m	£m	£m	£m	£m	£m
Operating cash flow	12.35	13.09	15.68	17.27	21.46	18.52

However, operating cash flow does not take account of important cash outflows that will need to be incurred to support the intended sales growth. In order to achieve the intended sales growth rates, fixed and working capital investment may need to be incurred.

Fixed capital investment is made up of two components, replacement and incremental. Replacement fixed capital investment (RFCI) is required to maintain the existing capital stock. Without maintenance and replacement the ability to meet current levels of demand let alone increases will prove impossible.

What about incremental fixed capital investment? Quite simply an estimate has to be made of the amount of incremental fixed capital that will be required to support incremental sales. One way to build this in is to assume that for every £ of sales to be generated some fixed capital investment will need to be incurred, albeit that it may not occur in even increments but may be incurred in "lumps".

There will also typically need to be an investment in working capital because additional sales will be difficult to sustain without incurring incremental working capital. More stock may be required and it may only be possible to achieve a growth in sales by extending credit and increasing debtors.

In common with incremental fixed capital it can be assumed that for every additional £ of sales to be generated, some working capital investment will be required. In other words, any increase in sales can only incur by taking on more stocks of raw materials and, possibly, by increasing accounts receivable (debtors). For purposes of our earlier example we will assume incremental fixed capital investment (IFCI) and incremental working capital investment (IWCI) to be:

Year	1	2	3	4	5	6
Incremental fixed capital investment	4%	6%	3%	2%	2%	2%
Incremental working capital investment	3%	3%	3%	4%	4%	4%

To find IFCI and IWCI in money terms, these percentages are applied to the change in sales receipts from period to period. Therefore, in Year 1:

Incremental fixed capital investment	=	(£105m - £100m) x 4%
	=	£.2m

and

Incremental working capital investment	=	(£105m - £100m) x 3%
	=	£.15m

Let us now pull all of this together to estimate prospective free cash flows. These are illustrated in *Table 5.4.*

Table 5.4   From after tax operating profit to free cash flow

Year	1 £m	2 £m	3 £m	4 £m	5 £m	6 £m
After tax operating profit	7.35	8.09	10.68	12.27	16.46	13.52
add Depreciation	5.00	5.00	5.00	5.00	5.00	5.00
Operating cash flow	12.35	13.09	15.68	17.27	21.46	18.52
RFCI	-5.00	-5.00	-5.00	-5.00	-5.00	-5.00
IFCI	-0.20	-0.63	-0.35	-0.38	-0.44	-0.50
IWCI	-0.15	-0.32	-0.35	-0.76	-0.88	-1.01
Free cash flow	7.00	7.14	9.98	11.13	15.14	12.01

As a result of having estimates for sales revenue today and knowledge of the five cash flow drivers we have shown how future free cash flows can be estimated. But how can the values for the cash flow drivers be estimated? Let us now consider this with reference to *Meunier plc*.

Estimating values for cash flow drivers

The usual starting point for estimating values for cash flow drivers, particularly when working with publicly quoted companies, is the information contained in the annual report and accounts. By way of an illustration we will draw upon the information contained in the Appendix to *Chapter 2* relating to extracts from the annual report and accounts of *Meunier plc*.

In the *Table 5.5* we have extracted key items relating to *Meunier plc* for the last three years. Further information is also provided about the depreciation for the year and RFCI.

Table 5.5   Historical data relating to Meunier plc

	1991 £m	1992 £m	1993 £m
Turnover	187.4	199.6	210.6
Profit before interest and taxation	20.2	14.7	12.1
Taxation	5.0	2.7	2.4
Tangible assets	66.9	76.2	86.7
Depreciation for year	4.4	5.2	5.9
RFCI	6.1	6.9	7.9
Working capital	20.5	16.8	9.3

Using this information we can calculate the five cash flow drivers for 1992 and 1993 as illustrated in *Table 5.6*:

Table 5.6   Calculating value drivers for 1992 and 1993

Cash flow driver	1992 %	Calculation	1993 %	Calculation
Sales growth rate	6.5	$\frac{(199.6-187.4) \times 100}{187.4}$	5.5	$\frac{(210.6-199.6) \times 100}{199.6}$
Operating profit margin	7.4	$\frac{14.7 \times 100}{199.6}$	5.7	$\frac{12.1 \times 100}{210.6}$
Tax rat	18.4	$\frac{2.7 \times 100}{14.7}$	19.8	$\frac{2.4 \times 100}{12.1}$
IFCI *	62.3	See below	77.3	See below
IWC	30.3	$\frac{(20.5-16.8) \times 100}{199.6-187.4)}$	68.2	$\frac{(16.8-9.3) \times 100}{(210.6-199.6)}$

*   The calculation of the percentages for IFCI is quite complicated in this case because depreciation and RFCI differ. They are calculated as shown in *Table 5.7*.

Table 5.7   Calculating Incremental Fixed Capital Investment (IFCI) for 1992 and 1993

		1992 £m	1993 £m
Net tangible assets at end of year		76.2	86.7
Depreciation for the year		5.2	5.9
Tangible assets before depreciation		81.4	92.6
Net tangible assets at beginning of year		-66.9	-76.2
Increase in tangible assets		14.5	16.4
Asset replacement (given)		-6.9	-7.9
Increase in fixed assets	(A)	7.6	8.5
Increase in sales	(B)	12.2	11.0
IFCI	(A ÷ B)	62.3%	77.3%

These values for the cash flow drivers based upon an historical review represent just the starting point. As we indicated earlier when we reviewed each of the cash flow drivers, a good deal of research is required to ensure that meaningful forward looking free cash flow estimates are produced.

Let us assume that the necessary research has been undertaken for *Meunier* which has been used to produce the cash flow driver estimates for 1994, 1995 and 1996 shown in *Table 5.8*.

Table 5.8   Cash flow drivers

	1992	1993	1994, 1995 & 1996
Sales growth rate	6.5%	5.5%	9% - expected end to recession
Operating profit margin	7.4%	5.7%	9% - expected recovery in profitability
Cash tax rate	18.4%	19.8%	20% - best estimate
IFCI	62.3%	77.3%	20% - benefit from past levels to be captured
IWCI	30.3%	68.2%	20% - estimate believed attainable from internal and peer group analysis

With a knowledge of these cash flow drivers we can readily produce free cash flow estimates by following exactly the same procedure as the earlier illustration. The result is as shown in *Table 5.9*.

Table 5.9   Free cash flow estimates

	1993 £m	1994 £m	1995 £m	1996 £m
Sales	210.6	229.6	250.3	272.8
Operating profit before tax and interest		20.7	22.5	24.6
Tax		-4.1	-4.5	-4.9
Operating profit after tax		16.6	18.0	19.7
Depreciation		7.0	7.0	7.0
Operating cash flow		23.6	25.0	26.7
RFCI		-8.0	-8.0	-8.0
IFCI		-3.8	-4.1	-4.5
IWCI		-3.8	-4.1	-4.5
Free cash flow		8.0	8.8	9.7

Relationship between cash flow drivers

In reviewing the cash flow drivers, factors that may limit future plans may be identified and there is a relationship between the cash inflows and outflows that it is important to recognise. To achieve sales growth expenditure will have to be incurred, the amount of which will depend upon the magnitude of the sales growth and the capacity of the business to expand.

The interrelationship between these cash flow drivers is vital to understand. The ability to achieve the targets set for one of them may well be dependent upon another, like for example the relationship between the sales growth rate and incremental fixed and working capital investment. Without adequate fixed assets and working capital it may impossible to achieve a 9% growth rate, let alone sustain it .

A real problem with fixed capital investment that needs to be recognised is that it may often be "lumpy", that is beyond a certain level of production it may be impossible to produce more without investing in completely new plant and equipment. Thus, the linear relationship between sales growth and investment is an assumption which may not always be relevant.

Forecasting the future can be very difficult and even when a satisfactory balance between the five cash flow drivers at last looks in sight it may well slip away. Why? Well, there may be yet one other limiting factor which, if it arises, will typically necessitate reforecasting free cash flows.

Quite simply, financing costs are omitted in determining free cash flows. Such costs in the form of dividends and interest are important and may often be subject to limited discretion. There has to be cash available to meet the perceived requirements of the providers of funds. In other words, a company typically has to ensure that sufficient free cash is available to meet financing requirements. This may well constrain ambitious plans such as that to achieve substantial future sales growth via the immediate purchase of plant and equipment and incremental working capital investment, if it results in unsatisfactory cash flows in the near term.

Value and free cash flow

Let us summarise the position we have reached. As regards determining value from cash flow data the focus of attention is upon free cash flow. In order to establish this free cash flow, which is defined as the cash available to the providers of finance, we have to deduct the cash needed for such investments in working capital and long term capital, from the operating cash flow. However, we saw in *Chapter 4* that to calculate value from cash flows we must discount them. Let us review the discounted cash flow approach discussed in *Chapter 4* with reference to *Meunier plc*, just to demonstrate how the estimated cash flows can be expressed in terms of a value today.

In *Table 5.9* we have estimated free cash flows over the three year period 1994, 1995 and 1996 to be £8, £8.8, and £9.7 million, respectively. To express these future cash flows in present value terms we need to discount them at the required rate of return (cost of capital). Let us assume that the cost of capital of *Meunier* after tax and when appropriately adjusted for inflation is 12%. With knowledge of this cost of capital we can calculate the present value of the cash flows of *Meunier plc* for the three-year planning period as being £21.06m:

Table 5.10   *Present value of free cash flows*

	1994		1995		1996		
Free cash flow £m	8.0		8.8		9.7		
12% Discount factor	0.893		0.797		0.712		
Present value £m	7.14		7.01		6.91		
Total present value	7.14	+	7.01	+	6.91	=	21.06

Concluding remarks

We have shown how to estimate free cash flows and some of the important issues associated with their estimation. Furthermore, we have shown how such free cash flows can be converted into a value using the NPV approach reviewed in the last chapter. What we have not yet considered is the time period over which free cash flows should be forecast and value estimated. This is the issue we address in the next chapter.

Appendix - Free cash flow and the cash statement

It is now a requirement for UK and US companies to produce and publish a cash flow statement as well as a profit and loss account and balance sheet. Such statements analyse cash flows under three types of activity:

> Investing activities: these include activities such as purchases and sales of fixed assets and investments.
>
> Financing activities: these include proceeds from share issues and loans, the repayment of loans and finance leases and the payment of dividends.
>
> Operating activities: these are defined as "all transactions and other events that are not investing and finance activities."

To take an example drawn upon earlier, the *BP Group plc* (and as is often so for other organisations) cash from operating activities is presented before investing or financing activities. In fact, in the *BP Group plc* cash flow statement there is a further breakdown into the following general headings:

	1992 £m	1991 £m
Net cash inflow from operating activities	3,494	4,240
Net cash outflow from returns on investments and servicing of finance	-1,186	-1,167
Tax paid	-507	-946
Net cash outflow from investing activities	-2,408	-3,262
Net cash inflow (outflow) before financing	-607	-1,135
Net cash inflow (outflow) from financing	245	1,054
Decrease in cash and equivalents	-362	-81

Cash flow statements like that for the *BP Group plc* do reinforce the point that like profit there are different measures and definitions. However, the information provided in such statements is not compatible with our requirements for strategic financial analysis. Our concern is always with free cash flow for which adjustments have to be made to operating cash flow for investment required to be undertaken, but *not* for any financing activities.

References

1. Burns T., "Riding the theme park rollercoaster", Financial Times, Monday February 14, 1994, p 15.

2. BP Group plc, Annual Report and Accounts, 1992.

6

Measuring Strategic Value

"Successful strategy is not the product of a vision, but of a very clear sense of the characteristics and distinctive strengths of the business that implements it."

John Kay

Introduction

Is the model of value we have developed so far complete? The answer to this is an emphatic no! The cash flows that we have been looking at so far have dealt with relatively short-term time periods. Strategic analysis inevitably deals with the longer term. Corporate strategies that deal with establishing a market share, building brand name values, or deciding upon the most beneficial areas for research and development need to be evaluated over the long term. It is vital to recognise that the most significant part of value can often be generated beyond the point at which managers are comfortable in forecasting, a point that will become clear shortly.

It cannot be ignored that once a market has been established, cash receipts could conceivably be indefinite - as long as marketing or research and development expenditure is undertaken to maintain market share. This may seem to imply that cash flows have to be estimated forever, which is an unrealistic proposition. Therefore, we have to look for ways of capturing future value as realistically as possible. We also need to recognise that different business units may well have different time horizons over which they need to consider their long term strategic plans. The time horizon, or planning period, is yet another variable in the evaluation of strategic plans. It may therefore be regarded as a *sixth* value driver.

In this chapter we will focus our attention around issues associated with the sixth of the seven value drivers introduced in *Chapter 3* - the planning period.

The planning period

One key issue that must always be considered in undertaking a business valuation is how far one should look into the future. In the case of *Meunier plc* we have looked at just three years in the previous chapter. Should we look further? If so, for how long? And, why would it matter?

In evaluating a capital project, normal practice is to select a time period that is consistent with the project's useful economic life. This is an area that is largely overlooked and in our experience time periods selected are often very arbitrary and not typically very long-term. For example, many organisations are loathe to extend their analysis beyond five years. Furthermore, as indicated at the end of *Chapter 4*, any value at the end of the time period used tends to be recaptured in assumed disposal values for fixed assets and the liquidation of stocks and debtors. However, for many strategic decisions a good case can be made for saying that an investment could have an indefinite life, providing any necessary capital expenditure, say for replacement, was undertaken. The argument here is that if an investment has been undertaken because a potential opportunity has been identified and, hence a competitive advantage, then this advantage will not necessarily be completely eroded at the end of the time period.

Let us put this within the context of one indicator of competitive advantage, the sales growth rate. An organisation that has identified the potential for substantial sales growth will eventually be limited in its ability to continue growing. Depending upon the conditions within the market in which it operates, like barriers to entry created by patents and trademarks, there will come a time when competitors' action will drive down the growth potential, and the likely premium able to be charged for products and/or services. However, a case can be made for assuming that the organisation will still be able to generate revenues and earn its required rate of return, if it ensures the quality of what it provides in the long-term is maintained by capital expenditure to replace old or obsolete assets.

The implications of this assumption are profound and need to be understood. *In evaluating any strategic option a potential case can be made for a very long-term, even an indefinite, cash flow stream, based upon <u>this</u> assumption that the quality of the underlying asset base can and will be maintained.* If this is so, it raises yet another important question - how can business value be calculated from a potentially indefinite cash flow stream? Does it mean that "forever" type net present value calculations have to be undertaken upon the basis of assumptions about cash flows into infinity? Fortunately, no! The principles of finance can be applied to the problem if we can separate infinity into two discernible parts - the planning period, and the continuing period.

The *planning period* can be viewed as being the period over which competitive advantage prevails which, in simple term we would equate with sales growth potential and the achievement of a positive net present value. Beyond this period lies the *continuing period* in which we will assume that no sales growth can be achieved. In terms of competitive dynamics we are assuming that a company able to generate returns above the cost of capital will eventually attract competitors, whose entry into the business will drive returns down to the minimum acceptable, or cost of capital, rate. In this continuing period the business will earn, on average, the cost of capital on new investments.

Strategic analysis and determining the planning period

One critical issue and one we are sure you have been wondering is - what is the correct time period for the planning period? A number of strategic approaches have been developed that can, in principle, be applied to determine the length of the planning period and, therefore, also the point at which the perpetuity cash flow starts. One commonly quoted within the context of business valuation is that developed by *Michael Porter* [1].

The planning period can be explained using five forces identified by *Porter* and illustrated in *Figure 6.1*.

Figure 6.1   Porters' five forces

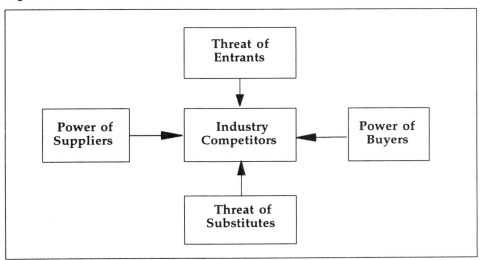

A company's competitive advantage may be threatened by potential entrants on the one hand and the possibility of substitute products on the other. It will also be affected by the relative power of suppliers and buyers and by the degree of competitive rivalry within the industry in which it exists.

In establishing the length of the planning period, a company's management needs to be aware of these forces. For example a company may be aware of certain potential entrants to the market but may also know that the barriers to entry are such that it will take a new entrant to the industry four or five years before it becomes a serious threat. Similarly, an organisation may be aware that in the market from which it buys its most important raw materials, mergers and take-overs are taking place which will make the suppliers' market less competitive and raw materials more expensive. Again, it is a question of judging the length of time over which the suppliers prices will rise .

Whilst the contribution by *Porter* has been invaluable, more recently the focus of attention within strategic thinking has been towards what makes firms different. As *Rumelt's* [2] work (summarised in *Chapter 1)* suggests, relative performance *within* an industry is a much more important source of profit than the industry itself. Thus, those organisations that focus upon relative performance should be able to generate the most value. It should be they who are able to benefit from competitive advantage, expressed in the Shareholder Value Analysis approach by a long planning period characterising good sales growth potential and free cash flows. The question is of course, what are these sources of competitive advantage?

As we indicated in *Chapter 1, Prahalad and Hamel* [3] have argued that competitive advantage is the consequence of the *core competences* possessed and nurtured by an organisation. These competencies can be thought of as being the collective learning of the organisation, particularly how to co-ordinate diverse production skills and integrate multiple streams of technology. Because of diversified information systems, patterns of communications, managerial rewards and so on, there will be an inevitable fragmentation of core competencies and an impetus for learning will be required via the development of a *strategic architecture*. Its purpose is to identify and commit the technical and production linkages across business units that will build upon distinct skills and capabilities that cannot be matched or easily replicated by other organisations.

John Kay has also sought to identify the core capabilities that can give businesses an edge [4] and he has identified four types of distinctive capability:

○ reputation

○ architecture

○ innovation

○ strategic assets

Reputation enables a company to charge higher prices, or gain larger market share at a competitive price, for a functionally equivalent product.

Architecture represents a unique structure of relational contracts within, or around the firm. Firms may establish these relationships with and among their employees (internal architecture), with their suppliers or customers (external architecture), or among a group of firms engaged in related activities (networks).

Innovation is a very strong source of competitive advantage, but one which is difficult to sustain because of the potential for replication. It also should not be ignored that innovation may be strongly related to architecture. For example, some firms have established an architecture which stimulates a continuous process of innovations. Other firms have created an architecture which enables them to implement innovation particularly effectively. Thus, the rewards of innovation may really be the product of the firm's architecture.

Strategic assets are sources of competitive advantage which are not based upon the distinctive capabilities of firms, but on their dominance or market position. An example is a concession to exploit a resource or an exclusive right to supply which is the product of the market, or regulatory environment.

These distinctive capabilities should enable an organisation to achieve what are often regarded as being major sources of competitive advantage - size, market share, market selection, and market position. However, these are the outcomes of the distinctive capabilities, which can be readily replicated. Their replication will likely only be associated with success if they arise as a consequence of a distinctive capability. They will add value only if their capability and distinctiveness are sustainable.

So what of the sustainability of these four distinctive capabilities? On the basis of his research, *Kay* suggests reputation as generally being the easiest to sustain, strategic assets as being sustainable over long periods if there are no changes in regulation or market conditions, and innovation the most difficult to sustain.

We are sure that it comes as little surprise to find that there is no simple rule of thumb to guide the length of the planning period for an organisation. From the research undertaken thus far is that it will depend upon a detailed analysis of its distinctive capabilities.

Free cash flow in the planning and continuing periods

For *Meunier plc* a planning period of 3 years was selected consisting of 1994 to 1996 inclusive and, given this, we can assume that 1997 and beyond corresponds with the continuing period. A breakdown of the components of free cash flow for both the planning period and the years comprising the continuing period are shown in the *Table 6.1*.

Table 6.1   Free cash flows for the planning and continuing periods

		PLANNING PERIOD			CONTINUING PERIOD		
	1993	1994	1995	1996	1997	1998	1999
	£m	£m	£m	£m	£m	£m	£m
Sales	210.6	229.6	250.3	272.8	272.8	272.8	272.8
Operating profit before interest and tax		20.7	22.5	24.6	24.6	24.6	24.6
Tax payable		4.1	4.5	4.9	4.9	4.9	4.9
Operating profit after tax		16.6	18	19.7	19.7	19.7	19.7
Depreciation		7.0	7.0	7.0	7.0	7.0	7.0
Operating cash flow		23.6	25	26.7	26.7	26.7	26.7
RFCI		-8.0	-8.0	-8.0	-8.0	-8.0	-8.0
IFCI		-3.8	-4.1	-4.5	0	0	0
IWCI		-3.8	-4.1	-4.5	0	0	0
Free cash flow		8.0	8.8	9.7	18.7	18.7	18.7

Because sales growth is assumed to cease at the end of the planning period, sales and hence operating profit remain the same in each year of the continuing period as in 1996. Similarly, with depreciation assumed to be unchanged, operating cash flow remains the same in 1996 as in each year of the planning period. However, where there is a noteworthy change is in the level of investment. Whilst RFCI remains unchanged because such investment will need to be undertaken to maintain the quality of existing assets, IFCI and IWCI fall off to zero. These you will remember were forecast upon the basis of sales growth - no sales growth, no IFCI or IWCI!

The result is that the free cash flow for 1997 and beyond is greater than that for 1996 by £9m, the value of IFCI and IWCI in 1996. But, whilst we know how to put a value on the free cash flows for the planning period, how can we value the free cash flows for the continuing period which may be assumed in principle to be received indefinitely? This question we will answer in the next section.

Annuity and perpetuity valuations

In the case of Proposal 1 in *Chapter 4* (NPV illustration *Table 4.2*) we saw that where the cash inflow is constant, the NPV can be calculated using the *annuity* approach. An annuity is a series of payments of an equal, or constant, amount of money at fixed intervals for a specified number of periods. So, for example in the case of *Meunier* if we knew that the £18.7m free cash flow was to be received for years 1997 to 1999 inclusive we could calculate the value of this constant inflow at 12% at the end of 1996 as follows

Value of annuity of £18.7m
    on last day of the   =   £18.7m   x   2.402   =   £44.92m
        planning period

The figure of 2.402 used in the calculation is the sum total of the individual present value factors for the planning period. However, the resulting annuity cash flow value of £44.92m does not represent the value today of the free cash flows for these three years, simply the value at the end of the planning period in 1996. To find its present value we have to discount it by the present value (discount) factor for 1996 of 0.712. Thus, its present value is £31.98m. And when combined with the present value of the planning period gives a total value of £53.04m (£21.06m + £31.98m).

If this is how we can calculate the value where the free cash flow is assumed to remain constant for a discrete time period, how do we calculate it when it is infinite? In fact, we apply the same principles as those associated with calculating an annuity but we consider a special case in which the cash flows are assumed to be received in *perpetuity*.

Our intention is to minimise the use of mathematical notation and only use it where it helps understanding. With this in mind let us consider the formula for calculating the present value of an annuity [5]:

PV of annuity = Payment $[(1\div1+k)^1 + (1\div1+k)^2 + ...(1\div1+k)^n]$

where, k = the discount rate (in the case of *Meunier* 12%)

Mathematically it can be proven that the perpetuity is a special case of an annuity and this formulae can be reduced to :

Perpetuity value = Payment $\div$ k

or, in terms of *Meunier*

Perpetuity value = Free cash flow $\div$ k

= £18.7m $\div$ 0.12

= £155.83

However, once again this assumes that the perpetuity is measured at the end of the planning period in 1996. It is *not* the present value of the perpetuity. As we saw earlier in our discussion of the annuity, the value of £155.83m at the end of three years is not the same as its value today. What its value is will depend on the cost of capital. Given that we know this to be 12% we can calculate the present value of the perpetuity by discounting it at the relevant discount factor, i.e. 12% at the end of year 3. Thus, the present value of such a perpetuity is found from:

PV of perpetuity = (Payment $\div$ k)(1 $\div$ (1 + k))^n

= (£18.7m $\div$ .12)(1 $\div$ (1 + 0.12))^3

= £110.95m

Seen another way £110.95m compounded for the next 3 years at 12% per annum produces £155.83m. To be more precise, in terms of our discussion in *Chapter 4*, £155.83m is the future value and £110.95m is its present value.

Now, the implication of this is that to arrive at a business value where there is a given planning period, the present value of the planning period has to be combined with the present value to be derived from the business beyond it. In the case of *Meunier plc* assuming a three year planning period and a cost of capital of 12%, the result is that the business has a present value of £132.01m (£21.06m + £110.95m).

The size of the value from the continuing period, often known as the *residual value*, is the largest contributor to total value. In fact, in this case the residual value represents 84% of the total value, hardly surprising when one considers that it represents a period of infinity, less the three years accounted for by the planning period.

The further into the future that the planning period extends the lower is the relative contribution made by the continuing period. But, does it make sense to value over such a long period? The answer is yes and there is good reason to when one considers the value of a share in relation to the cash returns by way of dividends and capital appreciation. A crude, but effective, indication of the long-term nature of share valuation is provided by the PE ratio. For example on Tuesday 22 February the FT-SE-A all share index had a PE ratio of 24.89, meaning that the average price might be simplistically viewed as reflecting 24.89 years earnings.

In summary, there are three important points to appreciate about the perpetuity residual value:

1. The value of the business is very dependent upon the cost of capital. This is because it is used in determining the perpetuity value which together with the free cash flows for the planning period, are discounted to a present value using a present value factor itself derived from the cost of capital.

2. The bulk of the business value comes from the continuing period, and for this reason many practitioners of the approach also look to methods other than just the perpetuity.

3. Related to the second point, the value is very dependent upon assumptions about the characteristics and length of the planning period.

Business value, corporate value and shareholder value

The value we have discussed so far and calculated for *Meunier* is what is known as *business value* and **not** shareholder value. Business value can be defined as the value generated by the free cash flows in which *all* providers of funds have a claim.

The concern within Shareholder Value Analysis is with the determination of that part of business value (and any other value) generated which is attributable to the shareholders. How do we find this?

Well to arrive at business value we discounted at a cost of capital that took account of the benefit of borrowed funds. Now we need to remove the present value of any such funds in order to find the claim on the value of the business attributable to just the shareholders.

It may also be the case that investments are held in other businesses, the benefits of which are not captured in the business valuation process. Any such benefits have to be added to determine corporate rather than business value. In fact, two adjustments are required to calculate shareholder value which take the following form:

Business value

+   Marketable securities or investments

=   Corporate value

-       Market value of debt and obligations

=   Shareholder value

÷   Number of ordinary shares

=   Shareholder value per share

In terms of *Meunier plc* we have estimated a business value of £132.01m, there are no marketable securities (e.g. interest earning deposits), and the notes to the accounts for 1993 show creditors amounts falling due after one year of £20.1m. If we take such creditors as being a proxy for the market value of debt and obligations we can calculate shareholder value as follows:

		£m
	Business value	132.01
+	Marketable securities	0
=	Corporate value	132.01
-	Market value of debt and obligations	20.10
=	Shareholder value	111.91

In Note 4 of the appendix to *Chapter 2* the number of shares for *Meunier plc* for 1993 is shown as 139 million. With knowledge of the number of shares this shareholder value can be converted into a shareholder value per share.

=	Shareholder value	£111.91m
÷	Number of ordinary shares	139m
=	Shareholder value per share	81p

What does this shareholder value per share represent? It is the estimated value per share which is very dependent upon the assumptions made about the seven key value drivers. Change any of these seven and so too does the value. For example, changing only the cost of capital to 11% produces a business value of £145.72m, a shareholder value of £125.62m and a value per share of 90p. The cost of capital is often one of the most important influences upon business value using a DCF approach, hence the importance of estimating it as accurately as possible. The issues associated with its estimation we consider in the next chapter. However, it is essential to recognise as early as possible the *relative* importance of *all* value drivers.

How might the figure for shareholder value be used? Well, for example, if *Meunier plc* wished to go for a stock market listing, this figure provides some indication of a target price per share for any share offering.

In the case of a company which already has a stock market listing, this share price can be compared with the publicly quoted price determined by the forces of demand and supply, to see if a *value gap* exists. This is the term applied to the difference between the publicly quoted share price and estimates of its value using specific company information. So, if *Meunier* was publicly quoted and had a market determined price per share of say 70p we have estimated a value gap of 11p at a 12% cost of capital (81p - 70p).

The implications of this value gap are that if a majority shareholding in the company could be purchased at 70p per share, the purchaser would benefit by 11p per share. Is this sort of approach adopted in practice? Well *Hanson plc*, the large UK conglomerate, reportedly purchased *Imperial Tobacco* for £2.5 billion. After selling off the group's *Courage* and *Golden Wonder* and other relatively small businesses for £2.3 billion, *Hanson* was left with businesses worth about £1.4 billion.

Why might such value gaps arise? One reason associated with conglomerates is known as conglomerate discount. This implies that the market discounts the value of a conglomerate's share price because, for example, of uncertainty about the ability of incumbent management to manage it as effectively as possible. It is the opposite view of the "big is beautiful" idea sometimes applied to corporations. More than one view was given of this being applicable to *ICI* before its decision to demerge into two companies.

However, let us pause at this point and reflect upon the figure for shareholder value we have estimated for *Meunier plc*. It represents the value derived from a very simplistic view of the company. Using seven value drivers which we have assumed to be constant and estimates for debt and other obligations, a figure of 81p has been calculated for shareholder value per share. In reality, not only would it be reasonable to expect that the future estimates some of these value drivers would have to be changed year on year, but also the degree of detail used in their estimation. For example, many businesses provide multiple services and/or produce multiple products. For them a more realistic process of valuation would be to calculate the cash flows relevant to, say, each business unit using planning periods that reflect the different distinctive capabilities of each, and then to discount them at a required rate of return relevant to each unit. All of these individual values could then be aggregated and the shareholder value estimated. The ability to be able to go into such detail depends upon information being available, which it clearly was not for *Meunier*. However, exactly what is achievable in valuing a multi- service/ product company, where access to information is not a limitation, we review in *Chapter 9*.

One other issue we raised earlier and which we should reconsider about the *Meunier* value is the proportion accounted for by the residual value. You may recall that assuming a three year planning period and a cost of capital of 12%, the resulting components of the business value of £132.01m were £21.06m for the planning period and £110.95m for the continuing period. The size of the value from the continuing period, the *residual value*, is the largest contributor to total value and represents 84% of the total value in this case. This sort of proportion is not unusual for estimates of the residual value when a perpetuity calculation is undertaken over short time periods. For this reason it is preferable to forecast as far forwards as possible.

Use of the perpetuity approach for calculating the residual value does cause concern among practitioners who, because of the relative contribution it makes to total value, may also use a number of other approaches. One that we will review in the next section, and which ties up with our discussions of traditional ratio analysis in *Chapter 2*, is the MB (market to book) method.

Calculating a Market-to-Book MB residual value

The process involved for calculating an MB residual value is to estimate the book value of assets that the business is expected to have at that time and then use a representative MB ratio to calculate an estimated market value of the company in so many years time.

Estimates of the MB ratio to use in calculating an MB residual value for an unquoted company like *Meunier plc* we demonstrated in *Chapter 2* with reference to peer group analysis. As with all methods assumptions have to be made and in this case it is likely to be that the current estimate of the MB ratio will not change with time. This may be a major assumption, because after strategic developments have taken place the MB ratio may well change, but it is very difficult to predict the future!

Let us illustrate the MB approach to calculating residual value using data relating to *Meunier plc*. To calculate the value of *Meunier's* assets in three years time we need estimates for replacement and incremental fixed capital investment , incremental working capital investment, and depreciation. Each of these has been estimated for the planning period up to 1996. In *Table 6.2* the assets at the end of 1993 have been used together with necessary adjustments to produce an estimated balance sheet value of the assets as at the end of 1996.

Table 6.2   *Book value of Meunier's assets*

	Fixed assets £	Working capital £
Balance 31st December 1993		
(from Meunier's Balance sheet)	86.7	9.3
Depreciation 1994	-7.0	-
Replacement 1994	8.0	-
Incremental additions 1994	3.8	3.8
	91.5	13.1
Depreciation 1995	-7.0	-
Replacement 1995	8.0	-
Incremental additions 1995	4.1	4.1
	96.6	17.2
Depreciation 1996	-7.0	-
Replacement 1996	8.0	-
Incremental additions 1996	4.5	4.5
Balance 31st December 1996	102.1	21.7
Total (Fixed assets + working capital)	£123.8m	

Note: Depreciation, replacement and incremental additions from *Table 6.1*

You can see that the book value of the assets of *Meunier* at the end of 1996 are estimated to be £123.8m. However, from this we must make a deduction for debt which has not taken into consideration in our calculations so far in order to estimate the book value of shareholders' funds.   Let us assume its value in 1996 to be the same figure as shown in the 1993 accounts. In this case the book value of *Meunier's* shareholders' funds will be £102.7m (£123.8m - £20.1m).

You may also recall from *Chapter 2, Table 12.7, item 11,* that estimates of *Meunier's* 1993 MB ratio using peer group analysis were 3.1, 2.3 and 1.5, depending upon whether the highest, mean, or lowest estimate was used. Using this information estimated values of the market value in 1996 are:

High	£102.7m	x	3.1	=	£318.37m
Mean	£102.7m	x	2.3	=	£236.21m
Low	£102.7m	x	1.5	=	£154.05m

These, of course, represent 1996 values which can then be expressed in 1993 terms by discounting them to a present value.

We are faced with a similar problem to that encountered in *Chapter 2*, which value to use!

Concluding remarks

We have now completed the valuation process to arrive at a measure which has come to be known as shareholder value. But, it need not be restricted in application to just this group of stakeholders, hence our emphasis upon *Strategic Value Analysis*.

Strategic Value Analysis is essentially a discounted cash flow valuation approach which differs substantially from many approaches because strategic issues are clearly incorporated. Think of it as being a financial tool, the application of which does not have to be restricted to the corporate "for profit" environment. Organisations of all types have to make strategic decisions involving cash inflows and outflows and need to meet a return required by providers of funds.

A critical point brought out in this chapter concerns the assumptions used in arriving at any valuation. Garbage in can all too easily be reflected by garbage out. It is critical to ensure that data and assumptions used are as appropriate as possible.

One key assumption within the approach concerns the required rate of return, or the cost of capital. This is often one of the most significant contributor to value, hence the need to understand its calculation as fully as possible. It is to this issue that we turn in the next chapter.

Appendix - Alternative measures of Shareholder Value

There is more than one view about how shareholder value may be calculated. In this appendix we review alternative measures and, most notably, Economic Value Added (EVA).

EVA is an approach based upon exactly the same underlying theory as Shareholder Value (SV) - it simply draws the component parts together slightly differently. Let us review the two approaches and illustrate how they produce the same conclusion with reference to a numerical example.

Previously we have shown how SV at its simplest can be thought of in terms of the following seven value drivers:

1. Sales growth rate

2. Operating profit margin

3. Cash tax rate

4. Fixed capital needs

5. Working capital needs

6. Cost of capital

7. Planning period

With knowledge of these seven and given information about the current sales revenue, the market value of debt, and the value of marketable securities an SV can be undertaken.

In fact, EVA can be thought of in terms of these seven value drivers, but draws them together somewhat differently. The steps in its calculation can be thought of as follows:

1. Using current sales revenue and the first three SV value drivers, calculate operating profit. If it is assumed that depreciation and capital expenditure for purposes of replacement are identical then this operating profit must also equal the operating cash flow.

2. Calculate operating profit/cash flow as a % of capital employed. For this "opening capital employed" is required for each time period which also requires making estimates of additional (incremental) fixed and working capital needs. These estimates can be made using value drivers four and five from the SV model.

3. Calculate the cost of capital, SV value driver six. For this exactly the same issues need to be addressed for both EVA and SV.

4. Calculate the "performance spread", that is the difference between the operating profit/cash flow as a % of capital employed and the cost of capital.

5. Multiply the performance spread by the opening capital for each year of the planning period (SV value driver seven) to find the individual EVAs.

6. Discount the individual EVAs at the cost of capital and sum them to find the present value of the total EVA for the planning period.

7. Determine the residual/continuing value using the perpetuity or any other more relevant approach and discount it to a present value.

8. Sum the present value of the EVAs for the planning period, the present value of the residual/continuing value and the opening capital.

9. Adjust the total value by deducting the market value of any debt and adding the value of any marketable securities.

10. The resulting value, which can be shown to be the same as the value resulting from an SV calculation, can then be divided by the number of shares if a limited liability company to give a value per share. For a quoted company this can then be compared with the quoted share price to see if there is any evidence of a "value gap".

To see how these ten steps apply in practice and the similarity between EVA and SV let us consider the following example:

Sales value for most recent year: £1,500,000

Depreciation for most recent year and
assumed to increase by £5,000 each year
for the foreseeable future (and assumed
to equal replacement fixed capital investment):   £50,000

Financial position at end of most recent year:

	£'000	£'000
Fixed assets		500
Current assets	250	
Current liabilities	125	
Net current assets		125
		625
Long-term loan		100
		525
Share capital		450
Reserves		75
		525

VALUE DRIVERS

Sales growth rate	15%
Operating profit margin	10%
Cash tax rate	30%
Incremental Fixed Capital Investment (IFCI)	15%
Incremental Working Capital Investment (IWCI)	10%
Cost of capital	12%
Planning period	5 years

APPLICATION of VALUE DRIVERS - YEAR 1

Sales	=	£1,500,000 x (1 + 0.15)	=	£1,725,000
Operating profit	=	£1,725,000 x 0.10	=	£172,500
Cash taxes	=	£172,500 x 0.30	=	£51,750
IFCI	=	£225,000 [1] x 0.15	=	£33,750
IWCI	=	£225,000 x 0.10	=	£22,500

(1) Incremental sales £1,725,000 (Year 1) - £1,500,000 (Year 0, i.e. now) = £225,000

PROJECTION OVER 5 YEAR TIME PERIOD AND BEYOND

	Year 0	Year 1	Year 2	Year 3	Year 4	Year 5	Beyond
	£	£	£	£	£	£	£
SV							
Sales	1,500,000	1,725,000	1,983,750	2,281,313	2,623,509	3,017,036	3,017,036
Op. Profit		172,500	198,375	228,131	262,351	301,704	301,704
Tax		-51,750	-59,513	-68,439	-78,705	-90,511	-90,511
Depreciation		50,000	55,000	60,000	65,000	70,000	75,000
Op. cash flow		170,750	193,862	219,692	248,646	281,193	286,193
RFCI (replac t)		-50,000	-55,000	-60,000	-65,000	-70,000	-75,000
IFCI		-33,750	-38,813	-44,634	-51,329	-59,029	0
IWCI		-22,500	-25,875	-29,756	-34,220	-39,353	0
Free cash flow		64,500	74,174	85,302	98,097	112,811	211,193
EVA							
Opening capital (1)	625,000	681,250	745,938	820,328	905,877	1,004,259	1,004,259
ROC% (2)		19.32	20.38	21.41	22.39	23.31	21.03

(1) For Year 1: Opening capital £625,000 + IFCI £33,750 + IWCI £22,500

(2) Operating profit after tax ÷ Opening capital for Year 1:£120,750 ÷ £625,000

SV CALCULATION

Year	Free cash flow	PV of free cash flow	Cumulative PV	PV of continuing value (1)	Cumulative value
	£	£	£	£	£
1	64,500	57,599	57,599	898,581	956,180
2	74,174	59,117	116,716	922,282	1,038,998
3	85,302	60,735	177,451	947,506	1,124,957
4	98,097	62,390	239,841	973,324	1,213,164
5	112,811	63,964	303,805	997,887	1,301,692

add: Marketable securities and investments   0

Corporate value   1,301,692

less: Market value of debt   100,000

Shareholder value   1,201,692

(1) For year 5: Future free cash flow £211,193 divided by 12% and discounted at 0.567

EVA CALCULATION

Year	Return on capital	Cost of capital	Perform-ance spread	Opening capital	EVA	PV factor	PV of EVA
	%	%	%	£	£		£
1	19.32	12	7.32	625,000	45,750	0.893	40,855
2	20.38	12	8.38	681,250	57,089	0.797	45,500
3	21.41	12	9.41	745,938	70,193	0.712	49,977
4	22.38	12	10.39	820,328	85,232	0.636	54,208
5	23.31	12	11.31	905,877	102,455	0.567	58,092
6+	21.03	12	9.03	1,004,259	90,685		
					÷ 0.12		428,486

Premium   677,118

Opening capital   625,000

Intrinsic operating value   1,302,118

add: Marketable securities   0

Intrinsic total value   1,302,118

less: Market value of debt   100,000

Intrinsic common equity value   1,202,118

The value determined using both SV and EVA should be the same. In this case there is a difference because we have chosen to show each step in the calculations which has made it necessary to round numbers to a manageable number of decimal places. Without such restriction the SV and EVA would both equal £1,202,428. What is important to understand is that there is a difference in the way the same value is calculated. SV is reliant upon determining a free cash flow profile into the future which is discounted to a present value. For deriving value at the end of the period covered by the forecast a perpetuity value can be calculated, although for some businesses other methods may be appropriate.

By comparison, EVA derives the total value by determining a performance spread, that is the excess of the return on capital above the cost of capital, which when multiplied by the opening capital produces the economic value added for each period in the forecast. These individual EVAs are then discounted and summed to produce a premium. This premium plus the opening capital is fundamental in determining the intrinsic common equity value. Businesses capable of earning more than their cost of capital produce positive EVAs and build premiums into their market values. Conversely, businesses whose returns fall short of the cost of capital generate negative EVAs and thus discount the value of the capital they employ.

EVA has many traits which liken it to conventional accounting approaches. Its emphasis upon measuring return on capital means that a link is possible with the traditional hierarchy or pyramid of ratios. However, it is important to understand that it is in fact a cash flow approach. Operating profit and operating cash flow are one in the same by virtue of the assumption that depreciation equals replacement capital expenditure. For this reason operating profit can be compared with the cost of capital without criticism that accounting and economic principles are being incorrectly brought together. The result of this comparison is the performance spread, a vital part of the EVA framework.

Both the SV and EVA approaches have been adopted by a large number of companies but it is also as well to be aware of some other approaches for which the theoretical support is more tenuous. There are those who focus upon the spread between the return generated by a business and its cost of capital. If the potential return generated exceeds the cost of capital they would argue that shareholder value will be created. On the other hand, if the spread is negative such that the cost of capital is greater than the potential return, then value will be destroyed.

A real problem in theoretical terms arises when return is measured using an accounting based measure of return like return on investment rather than economically based measures such as those associated with SV and EVA. Measures like return on investment and return on equity have their origin in accounting and are reliant typically upon accounting rules for their calculation. Making a comparison between accounting based returns and the cost of capital are best avoided.

References

1.	Porter M. E., *Competitive Strategy: Techniques for Analyzing Industries and Competitors*, The Free Press, 1980.

2.	Rumelt R. P., "How much does industry matter?", Strategic Management Journal, Vol., No. 3, March, 1991, pp.167-186.

3.	Prahalad C. K. and Hamel G., "The core competence of the corporation", Harvard Business Review, Vol. 68(3), May-June, 1990, pp. 79 - 93.

4.	Kay J., *Foundations of Corporate Success: How business strategies add value*, Oxford University Press, 1993.

5.	Brigham E. F. and Gapenski L. C., *Intermediate Financial Management*, 2nd ed., Hinsdale, Illinois, Dryden Press, 1987.

General reading

1.	Rappaport A., *Creating Shareholder Value: The New Standard For Business Performance*, The Free Press, 1986.

2.	Stewart G. Bennett III, *The Quest for Value: A Guide for Senior Managers*, Harper Collins, 1991.

3.	Print C.F., "Measuring Value - Different Perspectives", Henley Management College, Working Paper Series, 1994.

4.	Mills R. W., "Accounting for Economic Development", Conference Paper -The Role of Accounting in Economic Development, International Conference, University of Botswana, February 22-26, 1993.

7

Estimating the Cost of Capital

> *"Unfortunately, there is a large deviation between
> the two ways calculating the of cost of capital"*
>
> *The Lex Column, Financial Times* [1].

Introduction

How do you know if a potential investment is really worthwhile? In every day life it is common practice to answer this question with reference to the rate of return that is required, expressed as a percentage. If you want to borrow or lend money there will be a cost or return associated with it.

What applies in everyday life also applies in corporate life. Somehow an organisation has to ensure that the opportunities in which it invests are those which will satisfy the returns required by the providers of funds. What is a return to the providers of funds will represent a cost to the company.

Given that the cost of capital can be thought of in terms of the return required by the providers, the next question is how do you measure it? Are there any financial tools and techniques that can be used to assist in its measurement? What are they and how are they applied? Are there any alternative approaches and what is current thinking? These are some of the key issues that we will address in this chapter, but please bear in mind that they have to be viewed in light of our observations in *Chapter 1*. What were these observations? Quite simply, the impetus for the approaches we will review for measuring the cost of capital came from corporate America which has a well developed equity market. But, what we need to recognise is that what is appropriate and relevant in such circumstances, may not be in others.

A major challenge to be addressed is how should the cost of capital be measured in other business environments. There is a simple answer in principle - the required rate of return should equate with the opportunity cost of the funds tied up, that is the return which would be achieved from their next best use. Whilst the principle may be simple, the practice is far more problematic, a point we will reinforce later in this chapter.

As we have indicated, the cost of capital is a cost to a company but to the providers of funds it represents the required rate of return that they will require. Such providers are typically not a homogeneous group with identical requirements and expectations from their investment. At one extreme they may comprise long-term debtholders seeking a secure and fixed rate of interest, whilst at the other they may be ordinary shareholders who accept that the return received is most likely to be contingent upon the company's performance. Somehow we have to capture all of these providers' requirements in one percentage rate of return which makes the cost of capital a real challenge to measure.

In fact, it is a real challenge to measure if it is to be completely useful. This is because there are different ways of calculating it at the company level. Whilst one single cost may be sought there are different ways of measuring it, each of which will give a very different answer. This was seen only too well in the UK in 1992 when the regulatory body for water OFWAT and the companies it regulated attempted to measure the cost of capital.

Each party using a different approach, each of which we review in this chapter, arrived at a very different answer. OFWAT calculated the proposed cost of capital by measuring dividend growth, the result being a figure of some 5 to 6 per cent. On the other hand, the companies backed by several independent experts arrived at a figure of some 9.5 per cent using another approach (known as the Capital Asset Pricing Model).

Such differences may often be the case and can have a material effect upon business value. This can be readily understood in terms of the Strategic Value Analysis approach we developed in the last chapter. The residual or continuing value, calculated via the perpetuity approach, often represents the largest proportion of total value and is critically dependent upon assumptions about the cost of capital.

That there are different approaches for trying to determine this required rate of return and that the overall required rate of return may comprise different component parts that have to be brought together, represent one significant problem. But yet another exists. This is quite simply that organisations will tend to have capital allocation procedures delegated to parts of the overall business.

In large organisations it is not satisfactory and typically undesirable for all capital allocation decisions to be made at the centre. It often makes sense to delegate the authority for making such decisions. However such procedures may also need to recognise that different parts of the overall business will need to generate different returns. Quite simply, if one part of the business is riskier than another, it should not be regarded as too surprising that this part of the business will have to achieve a higher rate of return.

Are there any other issues that you should be aware of at this point? Yes, it is all too easy to become challenged by the various approaches that have been developed for determining the cost of individual components that make up a corporation's capital structure. Nowhere is this more the case than the cost of equity for which, as we have already indicated, a number of approaches have been developed to try and capture the rate of return required by shareholders. These approaches in themselves are challenging and important to consider but there is one other important issue to keep at the back of your mind. Any approach is *only as good as the data on which it is based.* You should not lose sight of the fact that the approaches developed to measure the cost of capital are heavily reliant upon historical data. This is important to bear in mind because the business world of today is turbulent and it is questionable how far the past is an accurate representation of the future. A good example of this has been provided by two studies, one by *BZW* [2] and the other by *Dimson and Marsh* of the London Business School [3].

BZW in its 1993 annual equity-gilt study, which looks at returns from UK shares, government bonds and cash since 1918, showed that companies have not adjusted to lower inflation rates in their appraisal of capital spending. By all accounts companies seem to expect returns of 20-25% but they should be looking at a return of 10-15% before inflation.

Choosing too high a cost of capital reduces value and from a planning perspective may make management demand an excessive return from new investment opportunities. That this is so was confirmed by *Dimson and Marsh* who found that when considering new investment projects many companies are living in the past and seeking a required rate of return that is simply too high. As a consequence they run the risk of investing too little too late, and of failing to share fully in the economic recovery.

To our minds understanding the cost of capital is one of the major challenges for UK management. Those who understand it should be able to ensure that their organisations benefit. However, as you will see from what follows this measurement is by no means straightforward.

In what follows please do keep at the back of your mind the "scene setting" issues raised in *Chapter 1*. There we identified that contrary to much opinion the dependence that could be placed upon financial theory for an unquestioned body of knowledge was limited. This means that financial theory relating to the cost of capital is still evolving and should not be set in "tablets of stone".

Estimating the cost of capital

The information required to estimate the cost of capital is best understood with reference to the *Figure 7.1*.

Figure 7.1   Components of the cost of capital

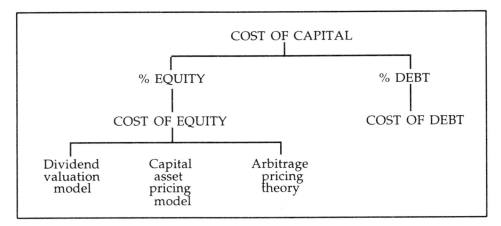

Determining the cost of capital is a difficult task. In what follows we will discuss its calculation using *Figure 7.1.* but we will start from the bottom left-hand corner and work. In broad terms, the steps we will follow are:

○ Estimate the cost of equity

○ Estimate the cost of debt

○ Determine the cost of capital by weighting the cost of equity and the cost of debt by the projected proportion of debt and equity in the capital structure.

Cost of equity [4-13]

The illustration shows three approaches available for calculating the cost of equity, the Dividend Valuation Model, CAPM and the Arbitrage Pricing Theory(APT).

Dividend Valuation Model

The Dividend Valuation Model considers that the return shareholders will require, and hence the cost of equity to a business, can be determined with reference to the future dividend stream they require. At its simplest, this approach takes the view that the cost of equity to a company is only the dividend it has to pay. Any capital gain relating to a share will arise only as a consequence of trading between buyers and sellers in the equity market, and will not involve the company itself. To convert this dividend into a rate of return it is expressed as a percentage of the market price of the share, i.e.

$$\text{Dividend yield \%} = \frac{\text{Dividend}}{\text{Price}} \times 100$$

However, this simple approach will not represent the cost of equity unless a very special set of circumstances apply, namely, that the current dividend per share must be paid out at the end of each year forever and that the amount of dividend must never change (i.e. never grow). This is an extremely unrealistic set of assumptions. Also, if the dividend yield is to be employed as a measure of the cost of equity, the company must pay a dividend and the approach is useless if current dividend payout is zero. Last, but by no means least, a low dividend yield implies a cost of equity capital that is less than the cost of debt - an unimaginable situation.

As an alternative you might encounter the earnings yield%, which is calculated by dividing the current annual accounting earnings per share (EPS) by the current share price, i.e.

$$\text{Earnings yield \%} = \frac{\text{EPS}}{\text{Price}} \times 100$$

It has the advantage of being "usable" even though a company may have no dividend payout. However, it leads to a number of difficulties. Not least among them is that it implies a negative cost of equity capital when earnings are negative. Also, it may lead one to conclude that for high price-earnings ratio companies, which are often those with high rates of growth, the cost of equity is lower than the cost of debt - hardly a likely situation. Equity in a geared company, being a residual claimant, is always more risky than debt. Finally, it relies upon accounting information, which may not reflect the underlying economic value of the business. Different costs of equity could be determined for the same company depending upon, for example, the method of depreciation adopted.

The most likely Dividend Valuation Model you will encounter for estimating the cost of equity considers that it can be derived by assuming that a company's dividend per share grows at a constant rate forever and that the company's risk will remain unchanged. If we call K_e the cost of equity, the model is:

$$K_e \% = \left(\frac{\text{Expected Dividend}}{\text{Price}} + \frac{\text{Change in Price}}{\text{Price}} \right) \times 100$$

Since change in price divided by price is just a growth rate, K_e is typically expressed as:

$$K_e \% = \left(\frac{d(1 + g)}{P} + g \right) \times 100$$

where,

K_e = Cost of equity

d = Current dividend

P = Market price

g = Expected dividend or price growth rate provided that investors expect dividends to grow at a constant rate in perpetuity

Thus, if a company had a current dividend per share of 4p, a market price of £1, and an expected growth rate of 10%, its cost of equity would be

$$K_e \% = \left(\frac{4p(1 + 0.10)}{100p} + 0.10 \right) \times 100$$

$$= 14.4\%$$

This measure of the cost of equity is fairly popular, particularly for valuing preference shares where g reduces to zero. In this case, the calculation of a cost of equity is quite straightforward if the shares are irredeemable, that is the dividend is paid in perpetuity. For example, a 10% irredeemable preference share with a nominal value of £1 and a market value of £2 would have a cost (K_{pref} %) using this approach of:

$$K_{pref} \% = \frac{\text{Annual dividend}}{\text{Market price}} \times 100$$

$$= \frac{10p}{200p} \times 100$$

$$= 5\%$$

If the preference share is redeemable, such that the dividend is not paid into perpetuity, then an internal rate of return calculation is required. This is necessary to find the percentage which equates all future cash flows from dividend payments and the redemption payment with the current market value of the share. This is known as the *yield to redemption, yield to maturity,* or *yield* for short. (The calculation of a yield for an irredeemable financial instrument is demonstrated shortly with reference to the cost of debt.)

However, for calculating the cost of equity relating to ordinary share capital the dividend valuation approach has to be used with care. First, the growth rate *g* is a long-run growth rate over an infinite horizon, and as such is a difficult parameter to conceptualise. It relies upon accurate estimates of growth rates that can be reliably projected into the future - a daunting task given that few businesses have a history of constant growth. Second, the long-run growth rate must, by definition, be strictly less than the cost of equity, K_e. This can be demonstrated by rearranging terms to solve for the market price:

$$P = \frac{d(1 + g)}{K_e - g}$$

If the long-run growth rate is equal to the cost of equity, the implied value of the company is infinite. If *g* is greater than K_e, the implied value is negative. Both results are impossible. Third, the parameters of the model are interdependent. It would seem that a higher growth rate implies a higher cost of equity. However, this is not true because the higher rate of growth will imply a higher current share value. The net effect will reduce the cost of equity. But if one estimates a higher growth rate, how much greater should P become? The answer is unclear. Finally, the model provides no obvious answer to the question - what cost of equity should be applied when the company is considering projects of different risk than its current operations? For this we need another approach.

Capital Asset Pricing Model (CAPM)

Modern financial theory suggests that a better way to estimate the cost of equity is from the demand side. Rather than looking at what a company pays out, it can be estimated from analysing what return investors require when buying a share. And, in a nutshell, the underlying premise of the approach is the more risk an investor is required to take on, the higher the rate of return that will be expected.

Investors' expectations can be modelled in the form of risk and return, and CAPM helps in explaining the risk and return characteristics of an asset that cannot be diversified away. It is in fact in a class of market models called risk-premium models which rely on the assumption that every individual holding a risky security will demand a return in excess of the return they would receive from a risk-free security. This excess return is the premium to compensate the investor for their risk. Put in everyday terms, a UK investor could invest in UK government securities which are reckoned to be risk free. Logically this can be thought of as a benchmark against which to compare other investment opportunities - more risk will have to be compensated by more return.

Beta

The risk premium in CAPM is measured by the beta. This risk is called *systematic, market,* or *non-diversifiable* risk. This risk is caused by macroeconomic factors like inflation, or political events, which affect the returns of all companies. If a company is affected by these macroeconomic factors in the same way as the market is, then the company will have a beta of 1, and will be expected to have returns equal to the market. Similarly, if a company's systematic risk is greater than the market, then the company will be priced such that it is expected to have returns greater than the market.

Perhaps it is easier to think of the beta as being a relative measure of volatility, the relative volatility being determined by comparing a share's returns to the market's returns. The greater the volatility, the more risky the share is said to be which relates directly into a higher beta. For example, if a share has a beta of 2.0, then on average for every 10% that the market index has returned above the risk-free rate, the share will have returned 20%. Conversely, for every 10% the market index has returned below the risk-free rate, the share will have returned 20% below.

How are betas measured? The answer is by measuring the variance of an individual share relative to the variance of a market portfolio like the FTSE All Share in the UK, or Standard & Poor's 500 index in the US. The most common method of estimating beta is with standard regression techniques based on historical share price movements. The historical period or estimation period generally accepted is five years, using monthly returns. This standard method is used in the UK and is provided by the London Business School's Risk Measurement Service.

To obtain a CAPM estimate of the cost of equity two other pieces of data are required, these being the risk-free rate and the equity risk premium.

Risk-free rate

The risk-free rate represents the most secure return that can be achieved. Anyone wishing to sleep soundly at night could invest all available funds in government bonds which are largely insensitive to what happens in the share market and, therefore, have a beta of nearly zero. The risk-free rate within CAPM is theoretically defined as an investment that has no variance and no covariance with the market. This means a perfect proxy for the risk-free rate is a security with a beta equal to zero, and no volatility. To find a perfect proxy is a difficult task, in fact it is empirically impossible. So the best tactic is to find a proxy that meets these requirements as closely as possible. Government securities tend to be the best candidates, since the government in many countries guarantees payment.

Equity risk premium

The equity risk premium represents the excess return above the risk-free rate that investors demand for holding risky securities. The risk premium in the CAPM is the premium above the risk-free rate on a portfolio assumed to have a beta equal to 1.0. If an individual security is more or less risky, then it will have a higher or lower risk premium. The risk premium can be estimated in a variety of ways.

Ex-post or historical perspective is a popular way to estimate the risk premium, the rationale being that history is a good predictor of the future. When history is used the first question to answer is, how should the return be calculated? Returns over time can be calculated by a simple arithmetic or compound (geometric) average, each of which are interpreted differently.

A geometric average implies that investors use a buy and hold strategy with dividends reinvested and is an appropriate performance measure if they hold for more than one period. The arithmetic average is appropriate if investors buy and sell every period.

The choice of whether to use geometric or arithmetic measures depends on the perceived holding period of the investor. For example, if the holding period is assumed to be ten years, then the appropriate measure would be the average of a series of ten-year geometric returns.

A second issue when using historical information concerns the period to use. For example, data in the US begins in 1926, which sets a limit for the longest period of 67 years. Many argue that this is too long, since most investors' memories cannot recall the lessons learned in the twenties, thirties and forties. The period selected we believe should resemble the market over the investor's horizon as close as possible.

Research has revealed the market risk premium for the US and UK to be between 5.5% and 11% historically, depending upon the time period chosen and the method used, and approximately 3 to 4% taking a forward looking view.

Once the beta has been determined, together with the risk-free rate and the equity risk premium the cost of equity can be found from the following CAPM formulation:

Cost of equity = Risk-free rate + (Beta x Equity risk premium)

For example, with a risk-free rate of 9%, a beta of 1.5, and an equity risk premium of 4%, the cost of equity would be:

Cost of equity = 9% + (1.5 x 4%) = 15%

Unlike the risk captured in the beta, risk that is isolated to an individual company, but not the market as a whole is called *unsystematic, specific,* or *diversifiable* risk. Company-specific risk can be eliminated by company-specific action and it is an assumption of the CAPM approach that such risk does not have to be priced and compensated for. Why? It is considered that all investors can carry diversified portfolios. Investors who choose not to be fully diversified will not be compensated for the total risk of their holdings, because the only risk which is priced and compensated for in the market is systematic.

CAPM has gained considerable acceptability in recent years and a good illustration of its use is provided in the annual report of *The Quaker Oats Company* [14]. It demonstrates how the cost of equity has been derived using a risk free rate comprising the sum of the expected rate of inflation and a "real" return, above inflation, of 2 to 3 per cent. The company refers to the risk free rate used as being the rate for US Treasury Bonds, which are unconditional obligations of that government and are intended to pay a real return of 2 to 3 per cent above long-term inflation expectations. The company also published its risk premium as being 3.6%, this being the sum estimated as being needed to be added to the risk-free rate to compensate investors for holding Quaker's shares.

CAPM is not without its difficulties, a point we made in *Chapter 1*. One key concern is the extent to which market related risk can be satisfactorily captured in a single indicator, the beta. Empirical evidence has demonstrated circumstances in which investors demand a higher return from one portfolio than another when both apparently are equally risky by virtue of having a beta of one. The difference in portfolio returns cannot be due to differences in specific risk because diversification nearly eliminates such risk in large, well balanced portfolios. And, if the systematic risk of the two portfolios were truly identical, then they would be priced to yield identical expected returns in equilibrium. Otherwise, an arbitrage opportunity would exist: investors could purchase one portfolio, sell the other and reap a positive expected return on zero investment. The observed difference in returns between these two portfolios represents a difference in systematic risk that is not captured by CAPM beta and has been taken to show that it is an incomplete measure of risk.

Arbitrage Pricing Theory (APT)

In an effort to improve upon CAPM an approach known as Arbitrage Pricing Theory (APT for short) has been developed. The principle which underpins APT is that two assets that have identical risk characteristics must offer the same return or an arbitrage opportunity will exist. APT attempts to measure the various dimensions of market related risk in terms of several underlying economic factors, such as inflation, monthly production and interest rates, which systematically affect the price of all shares. In a nutshell, regression techniques are used to estimate the contribution made by each APT factor to overall risk. However, this approach is more complex than CAPM and not without some difficulties in terms of its application. This was recognised in terms of its application in the US where, for example, the monthly production figures published by the government are only estimates of true US industrial production. This means that they are "noisy" (contain random errors) and inaccurate (contain biases introduced by the data-gathering procedure and the government smoothing or adjustment process). Error thus arises because high quality data in the form of share prices is regressed against lower quality data.

Means have been devised to overcome such problems and to operationalise the approach by *The Alcar Group* and in fact their research has demonstrated a significant improvement in the explanatory power of APT over CAPM [15]. APT explains an average of 37% of total share movements versus 22% for CAPM. In statistical terminology, APT has an R-squared fit (also called a coefficient of determination) of 37% while CAPM has an R-squared of 22%.

Is beta best?

As we indicated in *Chapter 1* there are concerns about measuring risk using beta, despite the development of APT with its multi-factor approach. What really brought the issue to a head was the recent work by *Eugene Fama* which concluded that beta was the wrong measure of risk.

The situation is that these controversial empirical findings, when combined with a good deal of criticism of the Capital Asset Pricing Model, leave financial theory in turmoil. However, there is a view that it may be possible to understand what is happening. Those who take this view are using new mathematical chaos techniques to view the markets as complex and involving systems. At the heart of their search is a belief that you can unlock the secrets of any situation if you can get the right perspective.

Whilst the chaos school seems rather far afield from traditional finance, it is attracting much attention, but unfortunately those involved have tended to develop multidimensional market models which only a privileged few can understand. The plain fact of the matter is that because of their complexity, the models are simply useless to senior management. For this reason we are probably unlikely to see the death of the Capital Asset Pricing Model, or the efficient markets hypothesis.

As indicated in *Chapter 1*, some still believe that the principles which underpin the Capital Asset Pricing Model and Arbitrage Pricing Theory can still be applied. For example, *Roll and Ross* argue on the basis of their work that one cannot conclude that Capital Asset Pricing Theory is dead. In terms of or concern with value, the implications are that whilst the techniques associated with the theory as regards CAPM and APT may be limited, they can be made more effective operationally by using a robust peer group or industry average return as a measure of market related risk. This will also help overcome some of the acknowledged problems of the two approaches, which may be summarised as:

1. Both assume that the past is a good representation of the future, a view that is clearly flawed for businesses undergoing or which have undergone a period of substantial structural change.

2. Since beta is measured by regressing returns over a long period of time (usually 5 years), the effect of the change on the company's beta will be slow to appear. Thus, the historical beta of a company that has recently changed its exposure to risk may not be a good estimate of its future beta.

3. Neither approach can be used directly for firms, divisions or other business entities that do not have publicly traded shares.

Measuring the cost of equity in unquoted companies

One feature of unquoted companies and divisions of quote companies is that there is no market price for shares, thereby preventing either an earnings, dividend, CAPM, or APT cost of equity from being calculated. The question is then - how in such circumstances can a cost of equity be calculated? The answer is by determining betas using two other approaches which are known as *peer group* or *cross-sectional analysis* which can be applied to the projects, divisions, and firms of business entities both with and without publicly traded equity, and for businesses that have undergone substantial recent change. These approaches we will review in *Chapter 9*.

It is also worth noting that these approaches can be useful in providing more accurate cost of equity estimates for quoted companies. This is because cost of equity estimates based on betas for individual companies may often have large uncertainties. For example, for a company with a beta of 1 and an estimated standard deviation of .21 there would only be a two thirds probability that the real beta is between .79 (1.21) and 1.21 (1+.21). Furthermore, the resulting uncertainty in the cost of capital can have a tremendous impact upon value.

Cost of debt

The second step in calculating the cost of capital is to calculate the cost of debt. This can be thought of as the rate of return that debtholders require to hold debt, the question is - how do we find this return? Given that debt may be associated with a specified rate of interest, you might (unfortunately incorrectly) consider that this represents the return. In fact the return typically has to be calculated and to do this we draw upon the principles of discounted cash flow analysis we reviewed in *Chapter 4*, particularly that relating to the internal rate of return.

Figure 7.2   Step 2, Cost of debt

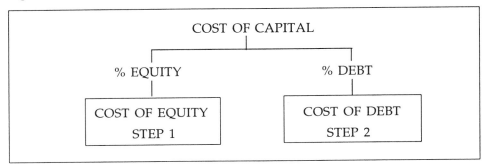

Yield

In *Chapter 4* we demonstrated that the internal rate of return (IRR) is the rate which equates the present value of future cash inflows with the outflows associated with the investment opportunity being appraised. There, we used *Figure 7.3* to explain this with reference to appraising a potential strategic investment opportunity.   And, exactly the same diagram can be used for explaining the return from debt. The IRR is the rate which equates the gross present value (of future cash inflows) with the capital outlay.

Figure 7.3   The yield

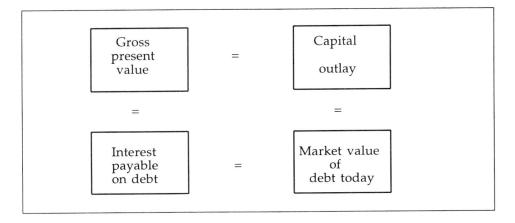

In *Figure 7.3*, the capital outlay can be thought of as representing the market value of the debt today. This value does vary and is best understood in terms of a large company with a stock market listing and which may well have publicly traded debt in the form of debentures, as well as shares. Via the forces of demand and supply the value of this debt will change.

The gross present value in *Figure 7.3* is the interest payable on the debt, the amount of which may often be quoted as a percentage of the nominal value of the debt instrument. So, for example, a debenture with a nominal value of £100 may pay 10% or £10 per annum. However, what this represents as a return to the investor will depend upon the price paid for the debenture in the stock market.   If say the value has fallen to £92, then the return or *yield* will have increased to 10.87% ([£10 ÷ £92] x 100). However, this does not tell the full story.

First, the debenture may have a redemption date. In other words, the debenture may return £10 for a fixed number of years, at the end of which there will typically be a sum of money paid by the company to redeem the debenture. If the debenture is to be redeemed after 10 years at its face (par) value of £100, then the yield is that percentage which equates an annual interest payment of £10 up to the point of redemption and the redemption of £100 payment in year 10 with the present value of £92. This percentage represented by **i** in the following formula, is 11.38:

$$\frac{£10}{(1+ i)} + \frac{£10}{(1+ i)^2} + \frac{£10}{(1+ i)^3} + \frac{£110}{(1+ i)^{10}} = £92$$

Second, the impact of taxation has to be taken into consideration.   One advantage of debt is that interest payments, unlike dividend payments on shares, are deductible expenses for tax purposes. This means that there is a potential benefit known as a *tax shield* from debt financing. How is this taken into consideration?   The relevant calculation is as follows:

Cost of debt after-tax   =   Cost of debt x (100 - Marginal tax rate)
                                 before-tax

Our example company with 10% debentures due for redemption in 10 years time and a marginal tax rate of 30% would actually pay out:

Cost of debt   =   10%   x   (100% - 30%)   =   7%

To convert this to the yield we undertake exactly the same calculation as earlier, but instead of using £10 for the annual sum we use the after tax figure of £7, and the resulting percentage is 8.2, i.e.:

$$\frac{£7}{(1+ i)} + \frac{£7}{(1+ i)^2} + \frac{£7}{(1+ i)^3} + \dots \frac{£107}{(1+ i)^{10}} = £92$$

So to summarise, the discount rate that equates the present value of after tax interest payment cash flows to the current market value is the cost of debt, and is referred to as the *yield to maturity, yield to redemption,* or the *yield* for short. For a company not expected to change its capital structure the cost of debt can be estimated as the expected yield to maturity of its outstanding debt.

Dealing with more than one source of debt

Typically businesses have more than one source of debt financing. In this case the overall cost of debt can be calculated by taking the weighted average of the individual instruments based upon market values. This involves multiplying the yield to maturity of each instrument by the percentage of the total market value of the portfolio that each instrument represents, and summing the products. This is illustrated in *Table 7.1* which concerns a real life example relating to a large US buy out:

Table 7.1   Calculation of weighted cost of capital

Type of debt	Column 1 Amount $millions	Column 2 Weight	Column 3 Yield %	Column 2 x Column 3
Short-Term debt	13,600	0.5199	11.27	5.86
Existing long-term debt	5,262	0.2011	9.75	1.96
Sub. increasing-rate Notes (Class I)Sub.	1,250	0.0478	13.00	0.62
Increasing-rate notes (Class II) senior	3,750	0.1433	14.00	2.01
Convertible debentures	1,800	0.0688	14.50	1.00
Partnership debt				
Securities	500	0.0191	11.20	0.21
Total	$26,162	1.0000		11.66%

Cost of debt after-tax	=	Cost of debt before-tax x (100 - Marginal tax rate)
	=	11.66% (100 - 35.5)
	=	7.52%

What happens when the cost of debt of non-publicly traded companies or divisions of publicly traded companies is required? Peer analysis can be used in which the focus of attention is upon peer instruments as distinct from peer companies.   The objective is to try and find peer instruments for publicly quoted businesses where the characteristics are similar. Quite simply in terms of the yield calculation we have discussed, what is not known for a non-publicly traded company or the divisions of publicly traded companies is the market value of their debt. This means that there are two unknowns, the market value and the yield, and a difficult calculation to say the least! Attention is paid in this approach to the estimation of the yield by comparing the characteristics of the instrument in question with those for publicly quoted companies .

Weighted Average Cost of Capital (WACC)

Nobody ever rationally pays more for anything than has to be paid. What applies to everyday life also holds true for corporate life and the calculation of the third step in the cost of capital calculation, the weighted average of the costs of debt and equity, reflects this view.

We saw in the last section that there is a tax advantage associated with holding debt. This might lead one to conclude that by relying exclusively upon debt a company could reduce its cost of capital. Up to a point this is so, but beyond a certain level of borrowing this advantage can disappear. Why? Well, there will be concerns from prospective (and existing) debtholders about the ability of the company to meet interest payment commitments. Also shareholders will require a higher return as a result of the risk to their dividends and potential earnings from having large prior claims from debtholders.

This view of potential tax related benefits of debt capital and "gearing up" on the one hand, and the disadvantages of increased risk on the other has given rise to the view of there being an optimal or ideal capital structure. That is there is some mix of debt relative to equity at which the tax advantage can be maximised before the perception of debt and equity providers is of greater risk and the need to be compensated for it by demanding a higher return. Essentially, the view is that once providers do require to be compensated with a higher return for more perceived risk, any tax benefit to the company will be at least offset.

Many believe that it is difficult to determine a single truly optimal capital structure in practice, but that it is more valuable to see this as corresponding with a limited range of possible debt and equity mixes. Irrespective of the exact characteristics of the capital structure, the real challenge is to locate where it potentially lies when taking a forward looking view. Remember that our real concern is to find the required rate of return or cost of capital to apply in valuing a potential opportunity characterised by a series of estimated future cash flows. This means that the cost of capital should relate to the future.

How do we establish this? Well, the answer is that we attempt to identify the most beneficial blend of debt and equity over the planning period. Typically, this will cause much attention to be paid to the most appropriate debt structure which will have to take into consideration conditions relating to both the economy and the business. For example, we know that perceptions and the reality of borrowing can change given different economic conditions. During the recent recession we saw a massive change in views about what constitutes an acceptable level of borrowing. Many individuals and corporations saw the upside of borrowing turn into a very real downside as interest rates rose at a time when effective demand and confidence were falling.

In addition to what is regarded as an acceptable level from a broad economic perspective, there is a need to consider specific business/industry characteristics. What does this mean? Well, different types of business have different types of asset structure. Those with more to offer as security should be able to benefit from debt financing. The same is also the case for businesses with a good track record, even though their tangible sources of collateral may be limited.

How is all of this information taken into account? The answer is by estimating a forward looking debt to equity mix in the form of a ratio (debt ÷ debt plus equity) which is used in conjunction with the costs of equity and debt discussed earlier to determine a weighted average cost of capital. Expressed as a formula the cost of capital is:

$$\text{Cost of capital} = \%\text{Debt}(K_d) + \%\text{Equity}(K_e)$$

where

$$\% \text{ Debt} = \frac{\text{Debt}}{\text{Debt} + \text{Equity}} \quad \text{(based upon market, not book values)}$$

$$K_d = \text{Cost of debt after tax}$$

$$\% \text{ Equity} = \frac{\text{Equity}}{\text{Debt} + \text{Equity}} \quad \text{(based upon market, not book values)}$$

$$K_e = \text{Cost of equity}$$

So, for example, if K_d is 7%, K_e is 12%, % Debt is 30% and % Equity is 70%, the Cost of Capital is:

$$
\begin{aligned}
\text{Cost of capital} &= (\%\text{Debt} \times K_d) + (\%\text{Equity} \times K_e) \\
&= (0.3 \times 0.07) + (0.7 \times 0.12) \\
&= 0.021 + 0.084 \\
&= 0.105, \text{ or } 10.5\%
\end{aligned}
$$

As can be readily seen, if neither K_d nor K_e changes, the greater the proportion of debt, the lower the cost of capital. For example, reversing the %Debt and %Equity produces the following result:

$$\text{Cost of capital} \quad = \quad (\%\text{Debt} \times K_d) + (\%\text{Equity} \times K_e)$$

$$= \quad (0.7 \times 0.07) + (0.3 \times 0.12)$$

$$= \quad 0.049 + 0.036$$

$$= \quad 0.085, \text{ or } 8.5\%$$

Being able to lower the cost of capital by this injection of debt could increase value massively if you consider it with reference to the *Meunier* example. However, the optimal capital structure argument means that any such attempt to gear up by this amount would be counteracted by at least corresponding increases in K_d and then K_e.

Strategic risk analysis

Risk analysis is a critical step in valuation analysis and if you do not try to capture it you cannot know whether value will be created or not.

As we have seen different types of risk should be dealt with in different ways. Broadly speaking, we have identified risk specific to the business which should be dealt with via the cash flows to be valued, and risk which is related to macroeconomic forces (systematic risk) and should be incorporated in the discount rate (cost of capital) in the ways we have described earlier in this chapter. Unfortunately such risks are not always dealt with in the manner we have described, and it is appropriate at this point to review the "do's and don'ts" associated with their treatment. Seven key points about strategic risk analysis have been identified and referred to as the "seven deadly sins" to avoid, which include [16]:

1. *Ignoring risk analysis completely.* Traditional accounting-based measures ignore risk which is dangerous because risk levels are too important to be ignored. If you do not know the cost of capital, including risk, you cannot know whether value is being created or destroyed. The solution is to calculate the cost of capital as illustrated in this chapter and use DCF techniques. When performed properly, DCF explicitly includes both systematic and specific risk

2. *Using a single cost of capital to evaluate all business units' strategies and acquisitions.* A US survey showed that roughly one third of Fortune 1,000 companies in the US used a single cost of capital [17]. The problem is that this overstates the riskiness of low risk units leaving managers with what has been termed a "lie or die" choice, that is either lie about the real situation, or have no future investment and growth. This could result in strategic liquidation of the business unit. It also understates the riskiness of risky units, resulting in a strategic over investment in risky units, potential value destruction

and a riskier company as time goes on. The solution is to use the matching principle, that is the cost of capital should reflect the systematic risk of the cash flows that are being discounted.

3. *Adding "extra points" to the cost of capital just to be safe.* All too often reasons for adding a premium sound logical and appropriately conservative. For example, it may be argued that a premium will ensure that approved projects will create value, will correct for overly optimistic cash flow forecasts and motivate managers to find better investments. However, over time only riskier projects will meet the higher hurdle rate with the ironic result that the firm becomes more and more risky over time! The solution is to make the best effort possible to develop an accurate risk estimate and use it.

4. *Using a cost of capital that reflects total risk rather than just the systematic risk that investors cannot diversify away.* The key point is that because specific risk can be diversified by investors, only systematic risk affects the cost of capital. Hence, inclusion of both types within the cost of capital calculation is incorrect. However, there is probably a good reason why this sin is committed. While most managers have a good intuition for their business' total risk, systematic risk is difficult to estimate. Nevertheless, a distinction should be made between the two   categories of risk, with specific risk being analysed using forecast cash flow scenarios and only systematic risk being built into the discount rate.

5. *Using the cost of investment specific financing as the cost of capital for that investment.* The same survey as quoted earlier showed that 17% of *Fortune* 1,000 companies in the US committed this error. It seems intuitive that the cost of financing a project would be its cost of capital. However, this ignores that over time, projects will be funded with both equity and debt according to the target capital structure. The solution is to use a weighted average cost of capital with a long term expected capital structure because it reflects the impact of a firm's strategy on the risk exposure of all investors.

6. *Using identical target capital structures for every business unit.* Like risk, appropriate capital structure can vary across strategies and business units. The only satisfactory solution is to estimate a target capital structure for each strategy/business unit using an approach we will develop in *Chapter 9*.

7. *Using book weights rather than market weights for computing the weighted average cost of capital.* In addition to the 17% in the US study that avoided this issue by using the cost of financing as the cost of capital, another 16% used book weights. The key point is that because investors have the opportunity to earn a return on the basis of market value, they do not have to settle for return on book value. Consider, for example, that you invested in a company that today has a book value of £5 per share and a market price of £10 per share. Would you want your desired return of 20% on the book value or the market value? Clearly since you could sell your share and earn 20% on some other similar risk investment, the return is logically based on market value.

Concluding remarks

Estimating the cost of capital is a complex, but very important business issue. As we have tried to identify many of the issues can be linked to assessing risk for which we have provided some guidelines. However, the cost of capital we have examined so far relates to a company as a whole. The reality is that most companies have units/divisions which may well have quite distinctive risk profiles and for which no single company-wide cost of capital is appropriate. How we estimate the cost of capital for divisions/business units we will consider in *Chapter 9*.

References

1.   "Cost of capital", The Lex Column, Financial Times, Wednesday, January 26, 1994, p.22.

2.   Urry M., "Expectations 'too high'", Financial Times, Wednesday, January 26, 1994, p.23.

3.   Dimson E. and Marsh P., "Unhappy returns", Financial Times, Wednesday, February 9, 1994, p.17.

4.   Fisher I., "Theory of Interest (1930)", Macmillan, New York and Hirshleifer J., "On the Theory of Optimal Investment Decisions", Journal of Political Economy, 1958, pp. 329-372

5.   Fama E. F., "The Behaviour of Stock Market Prices", Journal of Business, Jan 1965, pp. 34-105.

6.   Markowitz H., *Portfolio Selection*, (1959) Yale University Press, New Haven.

7.   London Business School Risk Measurement Service, Sussex Place, Regent's Park, London, NW1 4SA.

8.   Dimson E. and Marsh P., "Calculating the Cost of Capital", Long Range Planning, Vol. 15, No.2, 1982, pp.112-120.

9.   Mullins D. W., "Does the Capital Asset Pricing Model Work?", Harvard Business Review, January - February, 1982, pp. 105-114.

10.   Sharpe W. F., "Capital Asset Prices: A Theory of Market Equilibrium Under Conditions of Risk", Journal of Finance, September, 1964, pp. 425-442.

11.   Ross S. A., "The Arbitrage Theory of Capital Pricing", Journal of Economic Theory, Dec 1976, pp. 343-362.

12.   Fama E. F. and French K. R., "The Cross-Section of Expected Stock Returns" ,University of Chicago Centre for Research in Security Prices, 1991 and Fama E. F. and French K. R., "The Cross-Section of Expected Stock Returns", The Journal of Finance, June 1992, pp. 427-465.

13.   Roll R. and Ross S. A., "On the Cross-Sectional Relation Between Expected Returns and Betas", Working Paper #21, Yale School of Management, 1992.

14.   The Quaker Oats Company, 1991 Annual Report, p.35.

15.   The Alcar Group Limited, 1 Harcourt House, 19A Cavendish Square, London W1M 9AB.

16.   Eynon P. J., "Avoid the Seven Deadly Sins of Strategic Risk Analysis", The Journal of Business Strategy,Vol. 9 No. 6,November - December, 1988, pp. 18-22.

17.   Gitman L. J. and Mercurio V. A., "Cost of Capital Techniques Used by Major US Firms: A Survey and Analysis of Fortune's 1000.", Financial Management ,Winter, 1982.

8

Evaluating a Potential Acquisition

> *"Value, like beauty, is in the eye of the beholder."*
>
> *Anon.*

Introduction

For those at the very top of an organisation, typically the board of directors in a publicly quoted company the challenge is not only to ensure that the goods produced and/or the services provided satisfy the requirements of the market, but also the other stakeholders in the business. Further, for publicly quoted companies there is a *market for corporate control* which means that the share price has to be a key consideration and directors have to ensure value is provided. A failure to provide value to the shareholders may well result in a loss of control by the board and a drastic change in the management of the business as it stands.

What is important to realise is that there is no single view of value. The value of a business is what someone is prepared to pay for it, and unless their intention is to liquidate it and sell off the assets, its value will relate to what a potential acquirer is able to do with it. The value of the *Rover* car company to *BMW* was undoubtedly different to the view of value as part of *British Aerospace*. What is required is a means of evaluating any advantages (synergies) potentially available from combining two businesses. For this purpose Shareholder Value Analysis (SV) became well known.

In this chapter we will review how the SV approach can be used in the valuation of a company's shares before and after an acquisition, with a view to trying to identify the existence of any substantial value gap between different perceptions based upon the dynamics of business activities. We will illustrate how a large complex business with multiple divisions can be valued *in principle* using the SV approach where information about the detail of its activities is very limited.

Let us be quite clear at the outset that what follows is based upon publicly available information which we have shown to be limited in its comprehensiveness. This means that the valuation we have determined might differ substantially from that based upon expert knowledge of specific business segments, and information known to the company and not in the public domain. It is also important to recognise that the valuation we determine is based upon key assumptions about the continuance of the current status quo.

In practice when undertaking a valuation one should recognise that not only would the likely values of each value driver change over time, but also the composition and breakdown of each. For example, over the course of time the range of products or services produced or provided by a business will typically change, and it is therefore desirable to disaggregate the sales growth rate to reflect this. Similarly, over the course of time the cost of capital may well change to reflect the different expectations of the providers of funds.

What is the starting point in valuing a company? The answer typically is available published information such as the contents of its annual report and accounts which, as we demonstrated in *Chapter 5,* can be used to obtain an historical picture of past value drivers. This historical picture can then be used as an important base from which to make future projections. This approach was adopted in producing the case study covered in this chapter which was developed around events in December 1992 to January 1993 and which lead to the acquisition of the *Evode Group by Laporte.* The case will provide you with the opportunity to understand some important issues surrounding the acquisition, and to view the acquisition from the seller's and buyer's perspective.

Background - Valuation of Evode: Seller's perspective

In the new year of 1993, the Chairman of the *Evode Group, Mr Andrew Simon,* faced the prospect of having to mount a credible defence of his company against a hostile bid from the mini conglomerate *Wassall,* with more than a little difficulty.

The *Evode Group* was a small multi-national organisation which had experienced considerable growth since the second half of the eighties through acquisition, while its turnover grew from £95.8m (1987) to £279m (1991). *Evode's* businesses were broadly grouped in the speciality and industrial chemicals sector, and organised in five divisions:

- O   Adhesives and Sealants
- O   Industrial Coatings
- O   North American - primarily polymer compounds
- O   Plastics
- O   *Chamberlain Phipps* - footwear materials & components.

The *Evode Group* had been in some difficulty since it had announced the 1991 results at the beginning of the previous year. It had to reported a nearly flat turnover performance, actually down 6% from 1990, and profit before tax down 52% to £7.3m (£15.2m 1990) which after tax, extraordinary items and dividends payments, resulted in a loss of (£1.8m).

Evode's poor position had resulted from a number of factors:

- O   over exposure to the recession hit white goods and construction sectors in the UK.

○   its international markets, primarily US and EC, were effected by the world wide economic down turn.

○   overpaying for the acquisition of US company *Chamberlain Phipps* in 1989

○   the burden created by a high level of fixed payment capital, to finance the acquisition.

○   poor management, which saw reasonably high gross margins reduce to an average operating margin of around 2% on 1991 figures.

All of this left *Evode's* management with little credibility.

Evode's share price had slumped to a low of 43p in August 1992 but was beginning to climb again following successful rationalisation, cost cutting and marketing initiatives, to around the mid fifties.

This view of the company's share price can be reconciled with a valuation undertaken using a discounted cash flow (SV) model based upon published data shown in *Table 8.1*.

Table 8.1   SV Valuation of Evode

	Historical		Planning			Continuing	
	1992	1993	1994	1995	1996	1997	
	£m	£m	£m	£m	£m	£m	£m
Sales	239.90	241.34	243.27	249.35	258.08	267.63	267.63
Operating profit		20.03	23.60	23.69	24.52	25.42	25.42
- Cash taxes (33%)		-6.61	-7.79	-7.82	-8.09	-8.39	-8.39
+ Depreciation		7.10	7.50	7.90	8.40	8.90	9.50
Operating cash flow		20.52	23.31	23.77	24.83	25.93	26.53
- RFCI		-5.00	-5.50	-6.10	-7.30	-8.70	-9.50
- IFCI*		0	0	0	0	0	0
- IWCI**		-0.32	-0.42	-1.34	-1.92	-2.10	0
= Free Cash Flow		15.20	17.39	16.33	15.61	15.13	17.03
x Discount factor (11.76%)***		0.895	0.801	0.716	0.641	0.574	
= Present Value		13.60	13.93	11.69	10.01	8.68	

	£m
Cumulative present value of free cash flows	57.91
+ Present value of residual value****	83.12
= Corporate value	141.03
- Market value of debt and preference shares	107.51
= Shareholder value	33.52
Shareholder value per share (Divided by 72.71m)	£0.46

* To calculate the incremental fixed capital investment, multiply the forecast percentage by incremental sales. Replacement fixed capital is required to cover the cost of maintaining the existing plant and equipment.

** To calculate the incremental working capital investment, multiply the forecast percentage by incremental sales.

*** See *Table 8.2*

**** To calculate the residual value, take the residual period free cash flow, i.e. where there is no sales growth and divide by the cost of capital. Then use the discount factor for 1997 to calculate the present value of the residual value (17.03 ÷ 0.1176 x 0.574).

Table 8.2   Estimate of Evode's cost of capital pre-acquisition

Beta (B)	1.53
Equity risk premium (ERP)	4%
Risk free rate (Rf)	9.26%
Cost of equity $K_e = Rf + (B \times ERP)$	15.38
Cost of debt	11.055%
Cost of preference shares	8.14%

Capital structure

$$\%\text{Equity} = \frac{\text{Equity Market Capitalisation}}{\text{Equity} + \text{Debt} + \text{Pref.}} \times 100$$

$$= \frac{74 \times 100}{181.51} = 40.77\%$$

$$\%\text{Debt} \quad = \quad \frac{\text{Total debt}}{\text{Equity + Debt + Pref.}} \quad \text{x} \quad 100$$

$$= \quad \frac{41.9}{181.51} \quad \text{x} \quad 100$$

$$= \quad 23.08\%$$

$$\%\text{Preference shares} \quad = \quad \frac{\text{Preference shares}}{\text{Equity + Debt + Pref.}} \quad \text{x} \quad 100$$

$$= \quad \frac{65.61}{181.51} \quad \text{x} \quad 100$$

$$= \quad 36.15\%$$

Cost of capital = (15.38% x 40.77%) + (11.055% x 23.08%) + (8.14% x 36.15%)

= 11.76%

Other than the cost of capital, the following value drivers were used in estimating the shareholder value shown in *Table 8.1.* They were calculated from information which has been summarised in *Table 8.3.*

Year	1993	1994	1995	1996	1997
Sales Growth (%)	0.6	0.8	2.5	3.5	3.7
Operating Margin (%)	8.3	9.7	9.5	9.5	9.5
IFCI (%)	0	0	0	0	0
IWCI (%)	22	22	22	22	22

Table 8.3 *Summary of commentaries relating to value drivers*

"**Sales Growth Forecast** - 1992 figures suggests some signs of the recession lifting, and in particular strong growth in the North American polymer compound sector. In general sales growth will tend to be slow to flat until the recession ends and even then the effect may be lagged until core markets themselves grow. In 1992 Evode divested its footwear components business (*Chamberlain Phipps Division*) thus reducing its UK originated turnover by £31.6m.

Operating Profit Margin Forecast - average margins had improved to 5.7% in 1992 results. Divisional analysis suggests that the polymer business already has margins in double figures and adhesives and sealants have high gross margins which are being eroded. So *Evode's* turnaround strategy must seek to achieve a target industry average of 10-12% medium term. In the industrial coatings division *Evode* will be forced to keep margins low by the intense competition and depressed state of the market.

Fixed Capital Investment Forecast - *Evode* needs to balance its requirement to continue to invest in its successful businesses and restructure those that are not successful to produce higher margins, with the burden of servicing its debt. Therefore, it is expected that *Evode's* total fixed capital investment will not exceed the depreciation estimate for the five year period in line with its current policy. In fact, total fixed capital expenditure for replacement in the next five years has been estimated at £5m, £5.5m, £6.1m, £7.3m, and £8.7m, respectively. Replacement capital expenditure in the continuing period has been estimated as being £9.5m.

Incremental Working Capital Forecast - this is another area which may benefit from tighter financial controls. However, the effect of new marketing initiatives and severe competitive environment may force *Evode* into looser credit policies and higher than desired stock levels to maintain a good service which would force working capital expenditure up."

The buyer's perspective and the lead up to the acquisition

On 20th November *Wassall* launched a hostile bid for *Evode* with an offer of 80p per share (£58.2m).

Wassall was run by three ex-Hanson men under the chairman Chris Miller, and had recently successfully acquired two other companies in the sealants and adhesives sector. *Wassall* saw *Evode* as a basically sound organisation, with strong market shares in UK adhesives and coatings and US plastics, which would benefit from both being unhampered by gearing and the introduction of a strong management team.

Analysts had forecasted profits of £8.9m and earnings of 3.2p for *Evode* in 1992, and this confirmed *Wassall's* view that the company would be in a poor position to fund new capital expenditure, redemption obligations, repay bank debt and pay preference and ordinary dividends. In contrast its offer valued Evode at more than 25 times earnings and left Andrew Simon with little room to mount his defence. (On the announcement of the offer, *Evode's* shares jumped to 91p)

In his defence document, presented to shareholders on 4th January 1993, Mr Simon claimed that *Evode* was back on the mend and announced a 40% rise in pre-tax profits to £10.2m for 1992. However many feared the worst as the document omitted to include a profit forecast for the current year. Evode's shares rose to 103p and Wassall announced that it was not willing to overpay for any acquisition.

The SV assessment in *Table 8.1* suggesting a share price of 46p, confirmed that Evode had no options available to increase the group's value, otherwise the market would have recognised them and taken them into account. The two options that could have been considered were to:

- ◯   increase operating cash flows.
- ◯   decrease the cost of capital.

Increase operating cash flows - this option was not readily open to *Evode* in the midst of the world recession which was causing its principal markets to contract, and a high level of cash outflows to meet debt repayments could not be avoided.

Decrease the cost of capital - this option also offered little or no scope as the company was already highly geared with no chance of attracting new equity investment at its current level of performance and no way of generating extra cash to repay its debt (1992 annual report revealed that divestments had only managed to raise £10m).

Thus, the only strategic options seemed to be to sell the group or be acquired. But what was the right price to sell for? *Evode's* share price had already risen to 103p following the bid and *Wassall* had stated its unwillingness to overpay.

The view expressed by one analyst was:

> *"A range of 100p (realistic) to 120p (maximum)*
> *would appear to be the right ball park"*

This price was determined by analysing comparable peer group companies using gross cash flow multiples (share price divided by operating profit plus depreciation, and interest received)

Table 8.3   *Peer group - Gross cash flow multiples*

Allied Colloids	9.4
Brent Chemicals	5.4
British Vita	5.5
BTP	7.5
Croda International	6.0
Ellis & Everard	6.5
Hickson International	5.1
Wardle Storeys	9.0
Yorkshire Chemicals	9.0
Yule Catto	6.9
Average/mean	7.0

Cash flow multiples for *Evode's* peers in the sector were estimated as ranging from 5.4 to 9.4 with a mean of 7.0. Given recent difficulties it would be difficult to value Evode at the higher end of that range, particularly when its gearing is taken into consideration (debt and preference shares estimated at over 20% and 35 % of market value of capital employed, respectively in 1992). As a consequence the mean multiple has been used to produce the following estimated valuation of *Evode's* share price in which non convertible preference share capital has been treated as debt. Convertible preference share capital has not been treated in the same manner. Although conversion looks a long shot at present it cannot be ruled out and an allowance has been made for its conversion by way of a sinking fund to cover the potential liability of £40.7m in 9 years hence. This serves to reduce operating cash flow by £4.5m p.a.

Table 8.4   *Evode gross cash flow multiple valuation*

			£m
	Operating profit		15.6
+	Depreciation		6.7
+	Interest received		0.2
-	Sinking fund		-4.5
=	Gross cash flow		18.0
=	Gross cash flow per share		24.7p
x	7 multiple	(A)	173.0p

		£m
	Bank debt	28.5
+	Preference stock (US)	23.9
-	Allowance for 25% gearing	-8.3
=	Total debt	44.1
=	Debt per share (B)	60.6p
	Valuation (A - B)	112.0p

An alternative buyer's perspective, Laporte's rival bid

On 6th of January, *Wassall's* revised its bid to 95p per share and on the same day Laporte, the UK's second largest chemical group, bought 6.1% of *Evode's* shares at 100p and announced its intention to make a bid above 100p. *Laporte's* announcement effectively out manoeuvred what many thought would be *Wassall's* winning bid and allowed *Evode* to reject the 95p offer as inadequate.

Laporte's impending bid provided *Evode* with the opportunity of offering shareholders a good exit. But first *Laporte* had to come up with a new bid price, one which Evode would be able to recommend and be acceptable to Laporte's investors.

Laporte's appearance as a "white knight" was no sudden move as CEO Ken Minton had reportedly been tracking *Evode* for seven years, first approaching Andrew Simon in 1986 and again in January 1992 following *Evode's* bad results.

Laporte had a strong management team and had experience in transforming a low margin bulk operation into a speciality chemicals company. Mr Minton and his team had a reputation for ruthless cost cutting especially in non core businesses, and had overseen the rise in *Laporte's* margins from 10%-15% since 1986.

Laporte had five core businesses - organic chemicals, absorbents, metals and electronic chemicals, construction chemicals, and hygiene and process chemicals. Clear potential synergies were seen between some of these businesses and *Evode*. In fact, Ken Minton described the adhesive and polymer businesses as a "classic fit"

(*Table 8.6* provides an anecdotal record of *Laporte's* assessment of *Evode's* businesses).

As a result of detailed sector knowledge it was reckoned that the management of *Laporte* should be able to ensure that benefits from synergies could be achieved. Furthermore, it was believed that purchasing *Evode* need involve no dilution of earnings in the first year following acquisition.

Laporte offered and subsequently paid 120p for *Evode,* but was not prepared to assume any additional debt and, therefore, its offer consisted mainly of paper. The terms of its offer were:

- 23 new *Laporte* shares for every 112 *Evode* shares, valuing them at 120p, or cash alternative of 115p.

- 5 new *Laporte* shares for every 28 *Evode* convertible preference shares, valuing them at 104p, or cash alternative of 100p

Laporte raised £84.4m (15.4m new shares) via a placing and 1-for-10 open offer at 560p per share, 37.6m new shares were issued in total. 34m shares replaced *Evode's* ordinary share capital, UK and US preference share capital and debt with immediate interest savings.

Laporte's shares fell 27p to 583p on announcement of the terms of the offer, having fallen 10% since the announcement of its intention to bid.

Table 8.6   Assessment of Evode's businesses

Adhesives & Polymer Compounds Provide 'Classic Fit'.

Ken Minton, *Laporte's* CEO, was reported to have claimed that *Evode's* two largest business sectors provided great potential for synergies from incorporation into *Laporte's* businesses.

Adhesives & Sealants

Evode's operations have sales of £85m from the construction and automotive sectors. *Laporte* already sells different adhesives to the construction sector and uses an alternative distribution network.

Polymer Compounds

Although *Laporte* had no direct experience in this area, with sales of £85m, the products all involved formulating chemicals one of *Laporte's* strengths and therefore also provide a good fit.

The US operations were supplying high quality plastics to the food, medical and electronics sectors at good margins. The UK and Italian operations were in lower margin markets and required repositioning.

Question Marks Remain Over Other Businesses

Powder Coatings

With sales of £20m this area was outside *Laporte's* expertise and its potential for margin improvement limited, therefore would be under immediate divestment consideration.

Mr Minton said of the business, "When I have to compete with big boys like these *(ICI and Courtaulds)*, I start getting nervous."

Plastic Fabrication

Five operations with sales of £20m were also less attractive to *Laporte*. Three operations - in the US, UK and Italy - provided reasonable margins but the other two businesses required completely turning around.

Miscellaneous

Evode's remaining businesses, of which the vinyl coatings for wallpaper accounted for the majority of £40M sales, provide no fit at all for *Laporte.*

Acquisition must enhance Laporte's earning in the first Year.

Ken Minton was committed to immediate returns from *Evode* and promised to tackle their margins as his first priority. In the eighties Mr Minton had improved *Laporte's* margins from 10% to today's level of nearly 15%.

The improvement at *Evode* would probably come from:

- better pricing policies
- extending product ranges
- reducing raw material costs
- improved manufacturing
- cutting overheads
- better marketing
- significant job losses.

Mr Minton denied that he cost of rationalisation would affect earnings. *Laporte* had plenty of experience of cost-cutting and there would be few environmental costs.

Value of the acquisition to Laporte

A new SV calculation is provided in *Table 8.5* which forecasts a value of *Evode* to *Laporte* of £2.40 per share. This has only incorporated potential operating profit margin benefits and suggests that *Evode's* businesses will add value to *Laporte*. It also leads to the conclusion that the shares are extremely attractive at 120p per share.

Table 8.7   *SV Valuation of Evode to Laporte*

	Historical		Planning			Continuing	
	1992	**1993**	**1994**	**1995**	**1996**	**1997**	
	£m	£m	£m	£m	£m	£m	
Sales	239.90	241.34	243.27	249.35	258.08	267.63	267.63
Operating profit		30.17	30.41	31.17	40.00	41.48	41.48
- Cash taxes (33%)		-9.96	-10.04	-10.29	-13.20	-13.69	-13.69
+ Depreciation		7.10	7.50	7.90	8.40	8.90	9.50
Operating cash flow		27.31	27.87	28.78	35.20	36.69	37.29
- RFCI		-5.00	-5.50	-6.10	-7.30	-8.70	-9.50
- IFCI*		0	0	0	0	0	0
- IWCI**		-0.32	-0.42	-1.34	-1.92	-2.10	0
= Free cash flow		21.99	21.95	21.34	25.98	25.89	27.79
x Discount factor (12%)***		0.893	0.797	0.712	0.636	0.574	
= Present value		19.64	17.49	15.19	16.52	14.86	

	£m
Cumulative present value of free cash flows	83.70
+ Present value of residual value****	132.93
= Corporate value	216.63
- Market value of debt and pref. shares	41.90
= Shareholder value	174.73
Shareholder value per share (Divided by 72.71m)	£2.40

*   To calculate the incremental fixed capital investment, multiply the forecast percentage by incremental sales. Replacement fixed capital is required to cover the cost of maintaining the existing plant and equipment.

**   To calculate the incremental working capital investment, multiply the forecast percentage by incremental sales.

***   See *Table 8.8*

****   To calculate the residual value, take the residual period free cash flow, i.e. where there is no sales growth and divide by the cost of capital. Then use the discount factor for 1997 to calculate the present value of the residual value (27.79 ÷ 0.1200 x 0.574).

Table 8.8   *Estimate of Laporte's cost of capital post-acquisition*

Beta (B)	1.11
Equity risk premium (ERP)	4%
Risk free rate (Rf)	9.26%
Cost of Equity K_e = Rf + (B x ERP)	13.7%
Cost of Debt	6.9%
Cost of capital =	(13.7 x 75%) + (6.9 x 25%)
=	12.00%

More specifically, the impact of the acquisition on the drivers of value could be viewed as follows:

Sales growth - no immediate improvement because of the sales sensitivity to the economic cycle and the depth of the world recession.

Margin growth - the impact of Laporte's cost reduction initiatives may push margins up to 12.5% for the years 1993-95, but not as far as *Laporte's* average (14.2%) due the fact that *Evode's* products are of a less speciality nature. However, new overhead reductions from the total restructuring of the enlarged *Laporte* group (90 companies reduced to 20 business units) may cut a further 3% off the cost of sales and, therefore, increases operating profit margin to 15.5% from 1996-97.

Fixed capital investment - *Laporte* had been recognised by at least one analyst as being able to generate more profit from plant and equipment than *Evode*. This might well reduce the fixed capital investment requirement.

Incremental working capital investment - *Evode's* customers are likely to remain the same and to expect similar trading terms after the acquisition. Therefore no additional gains are expected to be possible here.

Mergers, acquisitions and external restructuring

The objective in undertaking strategic options like mergers and acquisition is to add value. Of course, additional value may not result immediately and it may take time to capture. This is where an approach reliant upon assessing future cash flows conveys distinctive advantages over more traditional measures that focus upon the shorter term. However, there will still be a major challenge to meet in ensuring that the additional value actually occurs!

How is value added from a merger or acquisition? Potential synergies may result, the benefits of which can be related to their impact upon seven value drivers of the Shareholder Value Analysis approach. For example:

1. Sales growth may improve because of being able to use the distribution channels of each organisation to sell the products of both.

2. Operating profit margins may be able to be reduced because of being able to use production facilities more efficiently.

3. Cash taxes may be saved by being able to plan the tax position of the new combined organisation. This area may be particularly beneficial for certain types of cross border deals.

4. Fixed capital requirements may be lowered by being able to use available spare capacity for providing for increased sales activity. There may also be an impact upon replacement capital requirements, a good example of this being the decision to merge by two high street clearing banks. It may be possible to provide service to both sets of customers in the new organisation by cutting the number of branches.

5. Working capital requirements can be reduced if the two businesses have a profile of cash flows opposite in effect to one another. There may also be potential benefits arising from better debtor, creditor and stock management.

6. The planning period may be lengthened because, for example, the new larger venture increases barriers to entry.

7. The cost of capital may fall if access is obtained to cheaper sources of finance.

A second, and very important source of value may also come from stripping out some activities/ businesses. In this way the costs associated with a merger or acquisition can be substantially reduced and the real benefits drastically improved. For example, as we illustrated earlier, the large UK conglomerate *Hanson plc*, after buying *Imperial Tobacco* for £2.5 billion and selling off the group's *Courage* and *Golden Wonder* businesses and other relatively small businesses for £2.3 billion, is reckoned to have retained businesses worth about £1.4 billion.

What makes merger and acquisitions particularly challenging is that obtaining good quality, robust financial information may be very difficult for an acquirer. On the other hand, for the organisation being acquired a major difficulty may be in terms of understanding the basis for the value placed upon the organisation by an outsider whose rationale might be based upon a totally different view of its future potential.

Concluding remarks

In this chapter we have illustrated how to value a quoted company using Shareholder Value Analysis. To obtain greater realism in the estimated value, valuations of individual parts of the business would preferably be undertaken. These could then be aggregated to form the total value. However, in order to do this requires an understanding of the one important part of the jigsaw puzzle that remains. You really do need to understand the relationship between risk and return within the various parts of a business.

It is possible, and indeed highly likely, that the returns demanded by providers of funds will relate to the overall characteristics of a business. Thus, a business involved in pharmaceuticals on the one hand and chemicals on the other (the case for *ICI plc* before its demerger) could expect providers of funds to base their required return from the company as a whole upon their expectations of the different business units. Change the structure of the overall business as the company did and, other things being equal, the required rate of return will likely change. There is a problem insofar as measurement of the required rate of return or cost of capital that we reviewed in the last chapter is based upon a holistic view of the company. What is really necessary is to be able to get behind this holistic view and measure the required rate of return for parts of the whole business.

Now the implications of this are vital to understand. In the conditions of business turbulence faced by organisations in the 1990s it is very unlikely that significant changes will not occur in the future as a consequence of reacting to business pressures and making proactive changes. This makes the need to be able to value individual parts of a business and hence how to calculate the cost of capital below the company level even more pressing. This we consider in the next chapter where we review how to estimate divisional costs of capital and the related issue of using strategic value analysis as a management, rather than a corporate planning, tool.

9

Strategic Value Analysis
a Management Tool?

> *"In sum, we have the tools to manage our company better from a strategic and financial standpoint."*
>
> *Brian Pitman, Chief Executive, Lloyds Bank plc* [1]

Introduction

You would be forgiven for thinking that what has been presented so far has all the appearances of being just an ideal tool for strategic planning and has little real relevance as a management tool. However, the approach can be used in managing the business, but this may have considerable implications for organisational culture, depending upon the extent to which it is implemented.

One simple way of understanding the extent to which value base approaches have actually been applied in practice is with reference to the following four stages of development:

Stage 1

Companies who do not appear to have experimented at all.

Stage 2

Companies who claim to be value oriented companies but whose actions belie this impression.

Stage 3

Companies who have adopted various value analytical techniques but not yet the broader managerial implications of the approach.

Stage 4

Companies who have embraced the underlying principles of a value based approach and who have embarked upon implementation.

The impetus to adopt the approach is often associated with some threat to the business which calls into question the structure as is. For example, a potential acquisition threat, like that of *ICI* by *Hanson*, might trigger questioning about the existing structure. For example, *Ronnie Hempel*, the Chief Executive of *ICI* was reported as saying that the demerger's aim was to allow *ICI* executives to concentrate on a narrower range of businesses, and to release what he referred to as "creative management energies" [2]. By all accounts the company's focus upon profitability in the past was less good than it should have been.

A second illustration of the impetus to adopt a value based approach can be related to one of the most noteworthy adopters of the approach in the UK, *Lloyds Bank plc*. The stimulus for the development of the approach came from a perceived need because of past performance and prospects for the future if no corrective action was taken. For example, ten years ago just before *Lloyds* embarked upon a shareholder value oriented approach its shares were selling at 66p, or 40% of book value: at the end of 1992 they were selling at 533p, or more than 240% of book value.

So, having recognised the need to adopt the approach, what in principle is involved in developing it as a management tool. In the first section of this chapter we will review the Critical Value Appraisal which represents the first step in developing Strategic Value Analysis as a management tool. This will involve a review of how to use the approach for assessing opportunities to restructure an organisation by taking advantage of all conceivable value enhancements whether they are internal or external. It is at this point that we have to recognise the multi-business nature of many organisations which introduces one other challenge referred to earlier - measuring the cost of capital below the corporate level.

In *Chapter 7* we discussed the issues important in the determination of the cost of capital from a corporate perspective which become even more complex when our attention is upon a business made up of a number of business units. As we indicated, each of these may have a different required rate of return, or cost of capital, that has to be determined.

However, before we proceed into the detail of this chapter, let us use an analogy with selling cigarettes and the issue of a health warning. What will be reviewed in this chapter concerns a good deal of detail associated with analysing value from a financial perspective. But, at the end of the day the financial perspective is only part of a total culture shift often associated with adopting a value based approach. *It is vital to recognise that a value based approach for managing the business will be dependent upon people to implement it.*

Critical Value Appraisal

So, let us assume that the trigger for a potential change has occurred and that a question has been asked about the structure of your organisation today and whether there is the need for possible restructuring. Such restructuring can take many forms and can involve a relatively simple change of focus from a product to a customer orientation, or can call into question business processes as a whole.

What clearly is required is some means of being able to judge whether in financial terms any benefit might result from an organisational change. To understand this a Critical Value Appraisal can be used. How the financial benefits associated with a potential restructuring can be measured may be thought of in terms of the following three steps which require the calculation of:

1. current market value

2. business value *as is*

3. business value with improvements

Let us review each of these steps.

Step 1 Current market value

The key purpose of this step is to establish the worth of a business as seen by the market. This provides a yardstick against which to measure your own valuations and, as you may recall, it was the approach adopted in evaluating the *Evode* acquisition which was discussed in the last chapter. It is calculated for a quoted company by capitalising the equity shares in issue, that is from the product of the number of shares in issue and the quoted market price of the share. However, it should be recognised that the value of the business as a whole may be greater than just this simple multiplication, because a premium would typically have to be paid to gain control. It is important not to lose sight of this premium for control because the quoted price of any share typically reflects only normal transactions in the stock market and not what would be required to gain control of the business.

For private companies and other organisations the process of determining current market value is even less precise. Peer group analysis of comparable quoted companies or companies with comparable characteristics may be necessary along the lines we discussed in *Chapter 2*, together with some other valuation approaches. A number of different valuation approaches would typically be used in recognition of the uncertainty caused by there being no informed market as such.

Step 2 Calculating business value *as is*

We illustrated in the last chapter how this step could be undertaken for the organisation as a whole, but this was a very simplistic view. In fact, this step is very difficult in reality because of the problem we highlighted earlier, that different business activities may be associated with different levels of risk, thereby necessitating the use of a different cost of capital to establish the values of individual business units. Despite this and other complicating factors that we will review, valuing a multi-business organisation *as is* involves the same basic principles that we have discussed in earlier chapters in relation to the organisation as a whole, the only difference is that a number of individual valuations for each business unit are required which then have to be consolidated. Furthermore, the most useful analysis will typically treat corporate headquarters in the same way as individual business units. Differentiating between business units and headquarters can be very useful, as we will show with reference to the identification of potential improvements for step 3.

The result of undertaking a valuation of individual business units and corporate headquarters will be a number of values which can be analysed and compared to provide an understanding of whether there would be any potential benefits from restructuring the business as a whole. In fact, the business units and headquarters can be thought of as being contributors to total business value which can be fine-tuned via operating improvements, sold to owners who are willing to pay a premium to put them to a better alternative use or to manage them better, or combined with business units of another organisation in an acquisition.

In what follows we will consider how to apply a value based approach at business unit level. Yet again we will focus upon issues and principles which can be readily demonstrated. What is far more difficult to demonstrate is the reality of such valuations which are typically far more complex in practice. So what are these issue and principles? They can be thought of in terms of the need to:

○ Define the main business activities to be measured

○ Collect data relevant to these activities

○ Undertake individual activity valuations

○ Aggregate individual activity valuations

Defining business activities

There are differing views about how to define business activities. One useful starting point is to look for the smallest practicable level of aggregation, that is the smallest collective unit that can be separated and viewed on a stand alone basis in its own right. How is this achieved? The maximum of independence between activities is the key to success and, therefore, the minimum of interdependence.

The definition of business activities may not be a problem if there are strategic business units (SBUs). However, this is not always the case and in common with our concluding remarks for *Chapter 8* it is preferable to look at a business in terms of its strategic risk, paying attention to those parts of the business that have distinct business risk characteristics. How can these be identified? First, identify the firm's SBUs, the guiding criterion for these being that each should ideally be a full competitor in an external market. Second, analyse each SBU to see if all the operations share the same business risk characteristics such as specific risks associated with, for example, markets served in terms of demographic and geographic segments and operating gearing, that is the same tendency of net profit to vary disproportionately with sales. (Operating gearing increases as the ratio of fixed costs to total costs increases, since variations in sales then produce much larger variations in net profit).

One other important issue worth raising at this point concerns the treatment of headquarters costs which can be thought of as falling into two categories, those necessary to support business units and hence attributable to those activities, and those which relate specifically to the headquarters. Those costs attributable to business units, e.g. providing services centrally that would otherwise have to be provided by the units, should be treated as business unit costs and not as headquarters costs. This distinction has important implications for the next step.

Collecting business activity data

The accounting system should be a good starting point for data, although it may often be necessary to reclassify it to correspond with the requirements of the analysis. For example, the business activities defined for strategic analysis may not correspond exactly with the definitions used in the accounting system. A classic area of difficulty concerns costs which may well be allocated and apportioned across the business in very arbitrary ways. You should also not lose sight of the observations made in *Chapter 3* concerning the data requirements for strategic investments. The most important point to be aware of is that some of the data costs relevant for accounting purposes may often be totally irrelevant in a future oriented business valuation.

Undertaking business activity valuations

This is often the most difficult part of the process and involves:

1. Identifying the relevant cash flows for individual business activities.

This can be difficult because various business activities may supply to one another and/or be supplied with goods from one another. Therefore, transfer pricing problems may represent a potential source of cash flow distortion. Where possible, transfer prices should be set as closely as possible to the market prices of any close substitutes. Why? Well, this reinforces the principle of viewing each activity on a stand alone basis. Related to this, corporate overheads must be dealt with carefully. Any overheads that would be incurred with the activity operating on a stand alone basis must be estimated and deducted in arriving at the relevant cash flow, e.g. accounting and computing costs incurred by headquarters on behalf of business units. However, those that would not be borne if the activities were separate should not be allocated.

2. Determining the cash flow costs and benefits of corporate headquarters

Those costs not easily allocable to business activities are those requiring close scrutiny at this stage. They have to be viewed in conjunction with the benefits to be obtained so that a position can be reached whereby the corporate headquarters are not seen to be either an ineffective burden relative to their cost, nor too lean to perform the role required of them. What is currently being spent upon headquarters? As a guide research undertaken on headquarters costs based upon 107 UK companies with between 2,000 and 20,000 employees suggested that headquarters are costing more than 1 per cent of sales, which often represents more than 10 per cent of pre-tax profits[3]. With this in mind, it is hardly surprising that companies have made major efforts to reduce headquarters costs in the last few years.

Whilst it is all too easy to focus upon cost-cutting when reviewing headquarters, the aim of reviewing headquarters should really be more ambitious and should focus upon increasing the value which the centre adds to the company as a whole. How is this achieved? The answer hinges upon tailoring headquarters activities more effectively to the company's particular strategy, structure, business portfolio, and top management style. In many cases that might mean cutbacks, but in others it will involve some increase.

3. Determination of relevant tax rates

The relevant tax rate for valuing independent business activities is that which it would pay were it not under the corporate umbrella. In a nutshell, the procedure to follow is to determine the taxable income of the stand-alone entity (including the headquarters) over the foreseeable future and then seek specialist help to ascertain relevant allowances and ultimately the rate to apply.

4. Determine the relevant cost of capital

We discussed key issues associated with the cost of capital at length in the *Chapter 7*. Here we will draw upon that discussion and place it within the context of a multi-business valuation.

Let us now review how to calculate the cost of capital for parts of an overall business, where the main problem is that there is no market price for shares, thereby preventing either an earnings, dividend, CAPM, or APT cost of equity from being calculated. The question is then - how in such circumstances can a cost of equity be calculated? The answer is by using two other approaches which are known as peer group or cross-sectional analysis which can be applied to the projects, divisions, and firms of business entities both with and without publicly traded equity and for businesses that have undergone substantial recent change.

Briefly, as we will demonstrate, peer group analysis is reliant upon the identification of an appropriate peer group of publicly traded firms in order to estimate the cost of equity. By contrast, cross-sectional analysis produces estimates of betas from underlying accounting information drawn primarily from the main financial statements of the business. This approach is reckoned to be less dependable for determining a cost of equity than either CAPM or APT, unless the business entity has recently changed its risk profile. However, it really does come into its own where the business is not publicly traded and particularly when no peer group is available.

Peer Group Analysis

In reviewing the use of peer group analysis to estimate the cost of equity we will use the following three step process:

Step 1: Identify the parts of a business which require separate estimates of the cost of equity.

Step 2: For each identify several peer group firms and calculate each of their costs of equity and gearing.

Step 3: Re-lever the peer group average to the target debt/equity ratio for the unquoted business.

In terms of Steps 1 and 2, you may recall from earlier that the starting point will often be with the identification of the firm's strategic business units, the guiding criterion for these being that each SBU should ideally be a full competitor in an external market. Each of these should then be analysed to see if all the operations share the same operating characteristics[4]. For example do they have the same:

○ product lines

○ end markets (defined by user attributes such as age, wealth and geographic location [5])

○ market share

○ total capitalisation

○ distribution network (direct selling, one or more intermediaries, and so on [6])

○ cost structure (percentage of revenue spent on materials, labour and overhead)

○ business strategy [7]

There is one simple message - try to find as many peers as possible! A firm's competitors often make the best peers, but within such competitors attention should be directed in particular towards identifying the sorts of similarities in operating characteristics we have outlined.

Once a peer group has been established from publicly quoted companies, the cost of equity for each of its members can be calculated using CAPM. This will typically contain debt and hence what we can refer to as financial risk. This debt related risk can actually be thought of in terms of increasing systematic risk and has a distorting effect upon what we really seek to find - business risk. In simple terms, business risk arises from business operations and has associated with it a return that shareholders require for bearing business risk which is known as the "unlevered cost of capital".

In recognition of the distinction between business and financial risk the cost of equity must be unlevered for each peer group member to find the unlevered peer group average. This peer group average then needs to be relevered to the target debt/equity ratio of the unquoted business. This relevered value represents the estimated cost of equity for the unquoted business.

Peer group analysis can be employed only when there are a number of publicly traded firms in the same industry. For firms in new lines of business this may not be possible. If a peer group is not available, then the only recourse is to cross-sectional analysis.

Cross-sectional analysis

This is an alternative method of estimating the cost of equity for an unquoted business entity. Cross-sectional models are also called "accounting" or "fundamental models". They produce estimates of CAPM betas called "fundamental betas" based on underlying accounting information. A proxy for the CAPM cost of equity is then calculated using the CAPM equation

$$K_e \ = \ rf \ + \ (Beta \ x \ Equity \ risk \ premium)$$

The bases for calculating this fundamental beta are accounting variables measuring profitability, turnover, operating characteristics, risk, and size. In addition, a link between the accounting data and economic factors may provided by including a cash flow coefficient in the form of the covariance of the company's cash flows with the cash flows of its economic sector.

Accounting variables that may be used in a cross-sectional model include:

- Total assets
- Cash flow coefficient
- Mean sales ÷ total assets
- Mean cash flow ÷ total assets
- Mean sales growth
- Mean dividends ÷ common equity
- Mean depreciation ÷ sales
- Mean inventories ÷ sales
- Debt ÷ equity ratio

The predictive power of this approach varies widely from industry to industry, and from company to company. It is likely to be far more accurate for companies where accounting data closely represents the value of the company than for companies where the economic value of certain assets is not represented by financial statements. For example, in industries like oil and petrochemicals many aspects are not well represented in their financial statements, and the model is likely to be less accurate. For example, the discovery of a oilfield may cause large swings in the value of a company's equity but does not show up in the financial statements until the potential value is realised.

Overall, a cost of equity determined by a cross-sectional model is less dependable than one determined by APT or CAPM unless the business entity has recently changed its risk profile. However, the cross-sectional model offers a good alternative when no peer group is available.

Calculating the cost of capital

Once the cost of equity has been estimated for each unit, a similar calculation is required for the cost of debt. How this can be estimated we reviewed briefly in *Chapter 7*.

The estimates for the cost of debt and the cost of equity can then brought together to estimate the cost of capital for each unit using the formula outlined in *Chapter 7*:

Cost of capital = (%Debt x Cost of debt after tax) + (%Equity x Cost of equity)

Aggregation of individual business activity valuations

By using cost of capital estimates for individual SBUs together with their forecast free cash flows a number all units values can be calculated. The sum of the values of these SBUs represents *total business value*.

If undertaken properly, this step will consist of more than just adding individual valuations together. There is enormous potential for error in undertaking the individual valuations which needs to be recognised. It is therefore wise to undertake some cross-checking by asking questions like the following:

- ○   Does the sum of the debts for individual business units equal total corporate debt?
- ○   Does the sum of individual business unit cash flows during the historical period approximate to corporate cash flows?

At this point you have to remember that it is all too easy to build a model that is flawed. Multi-business valuation is complex and will typically be undertaken using some sort of computer support, whether this is a spreadsheet or specialist business valuation software. It is wise to remember *garbage in, garbage out* at this stage because the aggregate value represents the base case or reference point for identifying potential areas of improvement.

Step 3   Estimate business value with improvements

By now areas of potential improvement that can be dealt with should be apparent, the value of which need to be estimated. For example, the potential benefits from cutting the costs of corporate headquarters is one obvious source, but there may be many others which may range from fine tuning on the one hand to drastic action, such as a major reorganisation, on the other.

As a result of extensive analysis it may be all too apparent that total business value cannot be improved sufficiently from internal action alone. Disposing of parts of the business may well be seen as being appropriate. In some cases, this may help to remove what has been referred to as *conglomerate discount* in the share price. This is where the extent of an organisation's diversification is seen as being almost a risk. The risk is that it may not be managed as effectively because of the breadth and often apparent lack of complementarity of activities. To some extent, this can be linked with our discussion of *ICI* earlier.

A disposal should only be undertaken if to do so will create greater value. Whilst an obvious point it can sometimes be very difficult to ensure that this is so. Measurement of the value to be gained starts from the base case *as is* which we discussed earlier. To this should be added the gain from its disposal, that is the difference between its market value as a stand-alone entity as operated by its current parent, and the market price when disposed of. From this value the tax liabilities created by its sale, and expected losses of benefits must be deducted. Some of these benefits may be difficult to measure accurately. For example, disposing of one business unit may impact upon all sorts of economies previously received such as deals with suppliers and the management of operations.

It is obviously important to search for all of the benefits and if you have a clear idea of who might be the potential purchaser you should attempt a valuation from its perspective. As we have indicated with reference to the take-over of *Evode* by *Laporte*, synergistic benefits can be very important.

Last, but by no means least, external improvements may warrant an acquisition. In this case establishing the benefits by way of synergies is crucial to success. The key message is to try and quantify all benefits as far as is possible using the approach we have described.

Having gone through these three steps the real underlying value of the business should be measurable. The difference between this and the market determined value for a quoted company, the *value gap*, represents what could be attained by a raider, or even by current management if it has the foresight and determination to make changes in good time. The best defence against a take-over is to ensure that the value gap between existing and restructured activities is so small that no outsider could reasonably gain from taking control.

Critical Value Analysis in context

You would be forgiven in thinking that we are still a long way from expressing Strategic Value Analysis substantially as a management tool. To reach this position it is important to understand that value has to be disaggregated. In effect, the seven value drivers we have worked with have to be manageable within a business unit context. This is not an insubstantial problem, and it is as well to understand that for many organisations intent upon applying a value base approach one of the biggest hurdles to overcome is how to develop it in a sense which is meaningful to the constituent parts of their overall business, often at a time when there is considerable change and reorganisation.

Some parts of the distillation of the approach are more straightforward than others. For example, the principles involved estimating cash flows are far more straightforward than cost of capital and planning period considerations. In practice, the determination of appropriate business unit costs of capital and planning periods are brain teasers to say the least!

How Strategic Value Analysis is being applied in practice

In the introduction we provided the following framework for understanding how Strategic Value Analysis has actually been applied in practice:

Stage 1

Companies who do not appear to have experimented at all.

Stage 2

Companies who claim to be value oriented companies but whose actions belie this impression.

Stage 3

Companies who have adopted various value analytical techniques but not yet the broader managerial implications of the approach.

Stage 4

Companies who have embraced the underlying principles of a value based approach and who have embarked upon implementation.

From our personal observations there would appear to be many companies who fall into Stage 1 and which as far as we know do not appear to have experimented at all. This, however, is an area that really does warrant some empirical research to see whether such impressions are correct. In terms of Stage 2 there seem to be many companies espousing the pursuit of maximising shareholder value in their annual reports but whose apparent interpretation of this would appear to be focused towards accounting based measures like earnings per share.

There are a number of companies that fall into the Stage 3 category but relatively few in Stage 4 for whom there is any substantial evidence that they have embarked on any broad based implementation. However, there is one good illustration of a company's experience with its implementation that has been recently documented and which we will review shortly.

Companies falling into Stage 3 and Stage 4 include a number of US companies like *Coca Cola, AT&T, Quaker Oats, Briggs & Stratton, and CSX*, which have adopted the approach. For example, *AT&T's* decision in 1993 to buy *McCaw Cellular* for $12.6bn has been reported as having been influenced significantly by valuation principles[8].

Unfortunately, very little has reached the public domain about companies' experiences in moving further forwards than the adoption of such analytical techniques and the broader based management implications of such approaches. However, as indicated in the introduction, one noteworthy exception is provided by *Pitman*, Chief Executive of *Lloyds Bank plc*.

Ten years ago shares in *Lloyds Bank plc* were selling at 66p or 40% of book value. At the end of 1992 the shares were selling at 533p, or more than 240% of book value. This ten year turnaround involved a number of steps which, when taken together, illustrated what can be achieved if the shareholder value concept is embraced.   What *Lloyds* seemingly did was:

○   Ranked its businesses on the basis of the shareholder value they had created.   Each activity was viewed either as a creator or destroyer of value and businesses with a permanent negative cash flow became a target for divestment.

○   It made provisions of about £3bn for problem country debt. This produced accounting losses but no movement in cash and as a result the share price went up, not down.

○   Higher value strategies such as expansion into life assurance and private banking reduced the group's risk profile and increased its cash flow.

○   It recognised that in measuring performance, "cash is king". Earnings per share and other accounting variables should not be used exclusively to assess performance, because they ignore the time value of money and exclude risk. This approach involved the inherent assumption that long term cash flows are what determines market value.

○   Because of greatly improved cash flow, *Lloyds* was able to finance capital expenditure of £2bn and a dividend increase of 320% over a ten year period.

○   The company introduced performance related remuneration, thus linking the interest of its people more closely with those of the owners.   More than 27,000 employees now own shares in the company and senior management have serious money at stake in shareholdings in the company and/or shareholder options.

The *Lloyds* experience indicates that Shareholder Value Analysis gave it a clear discipline. The company's goal has been to analyse every strategic decision in terms of its impact on shareholder wealth and it uses shareholder value analysis not only to evaluate acquisitions, divestments, capital investment projects, but also in assessing alternative strategies. As a consequence Pitman indicates that *Lloyds* knows which business are worth most to the company and how much value each can generate.

The company recognises that it now has the tools to manage its companies better from strategic and financial standpoint. Furthermore it has made some serious attempts in implementing the approach, but it also does recognise that it has a long way to go. Nevertheless, *Lloyds* has taken the approach very seriously and sees it as having an important part to play in the bank's future.

Key issues to consider in implementing Strategic Value Analysis

There are four main phases in implementing Strategic Value Analysis, which are the:

1. Introduction of concepts and gain commitment

2. Establishment policies and procedures

3. Integration of concepts into practice

4. Institutionalisation of the approach

Phase 1, the introduction of concepts and the gaining of commitment can take a long time. We would expect that take 6 months, if not longer, at minimum. It will involve:

○ Development and delivery of presentations to senior corporate and divisional management, e.g. overview of concepts and sample applications of its potential use within the company.

○ Discussion of key concerns and issues, e.g. linking value and executive compensation.

○ Obtaining commitment of the managing director and key corporate and divisional management.

Phase 2, establishing policies and procedures will often require considerable time and effort. In our experience, quite how much time is often dependent upon the size of the organisation, but as a rough guide six months can be considered to be ambitious. More specifically, this phase will involve the :

○ Formation of a "task force", e.g. drawn from senior central management and divisions.

○ Identification of specific obstacles and issues, e.g. how to relate the approach to the corporate financial management and reporting culture.

○ Determination of appropriate divisional costs of capital, residual value frameworks, and planning periods.

○ Development of appropriate applications at corporate and divisional level.

○ Development of application guidelines.

○ Identification of education requirements of those employees who will perform or need to understand the approach.

○ Development of education programmes.

Phase 3 is the longest and probably the most critical part of the implementation process. Nine months is a rough and ready guideline, the actual length of time also being heavily linked to the size of the organisation and how extensively the approach is to be introduced. It will involve the:

- Delivery of education programmes on the approach and how it links to current practices.

- Use of the approach for evaluating capital expenditure plans, acquisitions, research and development expenditure, and so on.

- Provision of expert assistance when needed.

The last phase, Phase 4, is very much an open book as regards the time involved. What it is likely to involve is the:

- Incorporation of the approach into performance measurement.

- Linking of the approach to incentive compensation schemes.

- Development of the approach for investor communications.

- Communication of the philosophy to all employees.

Challenges for the future

Strategic Value Analysis is vital in measuring whether value is being created or not. It is an extension of the application and principles of Shareholder Value Analysis, the importance of which we would not wish to underplay in triggering concern with how to measure value creation. However, Shareholder Value Analysis does focus attention very specifically upon one group of stakeholders in an assumed corporate setting. This is restricting because the principles of the approach can be extended to organisations of all types. If this is not immediately obvious, just consider that at its simplest what this approach requires is knowledge of future cash inflows and cash outflows, and the required return that has to be met. What types of organisation do not have to manage these three?

The extension of the Strategic Value Analysis approach to a range of alternative organisational settings remains a challenge as do two key areas we have highlighted. The first area is the cost of capital which, for the reasons we have outlined, is a major challenge and a major influence upon value creation or destruction - hence its importance. However, let us not forget the second and equally significant challenge, which relates to issues associated with determining an appropriate planning period. Organisations create value by having distinctive capabilities and it is from these that strategies can be most meaningfully be developed. How to identify them and then translate them realistically into the Strategic Value Analysis model is the real challenge.

The real creation of value comes from the strategies selected **not** from the method of analysis adopted. Strategic Value Analysis is just a financial tool (although a very important one) to facilitate sound strategic decision making - no more, no less.

Appendix - Unlevering and Relevering the Cost of Equity

Unlevering and relevering the cost of equity is achieved using the following formulae [9]:

$$\text{Unlevered } K_e \; = \; \frac{[\text{Levered } K_e \times (1 - \%\text{Debt})] + [\text{Rf} \times (1 - T_m) \times \%\text{Debt}]}{1 - (T_m \times \% \text{ Debt})}$$

where

$$\% \text{ Debt} \; = \; \frac{\text{Debt}}{\text{Debt} + \text{Equity}} \qquad \text{(based on market values)}$$

$$\text{rf} \; = \; \text{Risk-free rate}$$

$$T_m \; = \; \text{Marginal tax rate}$$

$$\text{Levered } K_e \; = \; \frac{\text{Unlevered } K_e + [(\text{Unlevered } K_e\text{-rf}) \times (1\text{-}T_m) \times \%\text{Debt}]}{(1 - \% \text{ Debt})}$$

where

$$\% \text{ Debt} \; = \; \frac{\text{Debt}}{\text{Debt} + \text{Equity}} \qquad \text{(based on market values)}$$

$$\text{rf} \; = \; \text{Risk-free rate}$$

$$T_m \; = \; \text{Marginal tax rate}$$

References

1. Pitman B., "Shareholder value analysis in action", The Treasurer, Special issue, March, 1993, pp. 14-17.

2. Abrahams P., "Relaunch into more enterprising culture", Financial Times, Thursday July 29, 1993, p20.

3. Lorenz C., "Size isn't everything", Financial Times, Monday November 29, 1993, p 13.

4. Hergert M., "Strategic Resource Allocation Using Divisional Hurdle Rates", Planning Review, January-February, 1987.

5. For example, the cyclicality and competitive structure of say the ice cream business will differ for companies operating in very different climates, e.g. Alaska versus Florida.

6. Kotler P., *Marketing Management*, 3rd edition, New York:Prentice Hall, 1976, pp. 275-302.

7. Porter M. E., , New York: The Free Press, 1980.

8. Tully S., "The Real Key to Creating Wealth", Fortune , September 20, 1993

9. Hamada R. S., "Portfolio Analysis, Market Equilibrium, and Corporation Finance", Journal of Finance, 24, 1969.

Present value of £1

Period	6	8	10	11	12	13	14	15	16	17
1	.943	.926	.909	.901	.893	.885	.877	.870	.862	.855
2	.890	.857	.826	.812	.797	.783	.769	.756	.743	.731
3	.840	.794	.751	.731	.712	.693	.675	.658	.641	.624
4	.792	.735	.683	.659	.636	.613	.592	.572	.552	.534
5	.747	.681	.621	.593	.567	.543	.519	.497	.476	.456
6	.705	.630	.564	.535	.507	.480	.456	.432	.410	.390
7	.665	.583	.513	.482	.452	.425	.400	.376	.354	.333
8	.627	.540	.467	.434	.404	.376	.351	.327	.305	.285
9	.592	.500	.424	.391	.361	.333	.308	.284	.263	.243
10	.558	.463	.386	.352	.322	.295	.270	.247	.227	.208
11	.527	.429	.350	.317	.287	.261	.237	.215	.195	.178
12	.497	.397	.319	.286	.257	.231	.208	.187	.168	.152
13	.469	.368	.290	.258	.229	.204	.182	.163	.145	.130
14	.442	.340	.263	.232	.205	.181	.160	.141	.125	.111
15	.417	.315	.239	.209	.183	.160	.140	.123	.108	.095

Period	18	19	20	21	22	23	24	26	28	30
1	.847	.840	.833	.826	.820	.813	.806	.794	.781	.769
2	.718	.706	.694	.683	.672	.661	.650	.630	.610	.592
3	.609	.593	.579	.564	.551	.537	.524	.500	.477	.455
4	.516	.499	.482	.467	.451	.437	.423	.397	.373	.350
5	.437	.419	.402	.386	.370	.355	.341	.315	.291	.269
6	.370	.352	.335	.319	.303	.289	.275	.250	.227	.207
7	.314	.296	.279	.263	.249	.235	.222	.198	.178	.159
8	.266	.249	.233	.218	.204	.191	.179	.157	.139	.123
9	.225	.209	.194	.180	.167	.155	.144	.125	.108	.094
10	.191	.176	.162	.149	.137	.126	.116	.099	.085	.073
11	.162	.148	.135	.123	.112	.103	.094	.079	.066	.056
12	.137	.124	.112	.102	.092	.083	.076	.062	.052	.043
13	.116	.104	.093	.084	.075	.068	.061	.050	.040	.033
14	.099	.088	.078	.069	.062	.055	.049	.039	.032	.025
15	.084	.074	.065	.057	.051	.045	.040	.031	.025	.020

Annuity of £1

Period	6	8	10	11	12	13	14	15	16	17
1	.943	.926	.909	.901	.893	.885	.877	.870	.862	.855
2	1.833	1.783	1.736	1.713	1.690	1.668	1.647	1.626	1.605	1.585
3	2.673	2.577	2.487	2.444	2.402	2.361	2.322	2.283	2.246	2.210
4	3.465	3.312	3.170	3.102	3.037	2.974	2.914	2.855	2.798	2.743
5	4.212	3.993	3.791	3.696	3.605	3.517	3.433	3.352	3.274	3.199
6	4.917	4.623	4.355	4.231	4.111	3.998	3.889	3.784	3.685	3.589
7	5.582	5.206	4.868	4.712	4.564	4.423	4.288	4.160	4.039	3.922
8	6.210	5.747	5.335	5.146	4.968	4.799	4.639	4.487	4.344	4.207
9	6.802	6.247	5.759	5.537	5.328	5.132	4.946	4.772	4.607	4.451
10	7.360	6.710	6.145	5.889	5.650	5.426	5.216	5.019	4.833	4.659
11	7.887	7.139	6.495	6.207	5.938	5.687	5.453	5.234	5.029	4.836
12	8.384	7.536	6.814	6.492	6.194	5.918	5.660	5.421	5.197	4.988
13	8.853	7.904	7.103	6.750	6.424	6.122	5.842	5.583	5.342	5.118
14	9.295	8.244	7.367	6.982	6.628	6.302	6.002	5.724	5.468	5.229
15	9.712	8.559	7.606	7.191	6.811	6.462	6.142	5.847	5.575	5.324

Period	18	19	20	21	22	23	24	26	28	30
1	.847	.840	.833	.826	.820	.813	.806	.794	.781	.769
2	1.566	1.547	1.528	1.509	1.492	1.474	1.457	1.424	1.392	1.361
3	2.174	2.140	2.106	2.074	2.042	2.011	1.981	1.923	1.868	1.816
4	2.690	2.639	2.589	2.540	2.494	2.448	2.404	2.320	2.241	2.166
5	3.127	3.058	2.991	2.926	2.864	2.803	2.745	2.635	2.532	2.436
6	3.498	3.410	3.326	3.245	3.167	3.092	3.020	2.885	2.759	2.643
7	3.812	3.706	3.605	3.508	3.416	3.327	3.242	3.083	2.937	2.802
8	4.078	3.954	3.837	3.726	3.619	3.58	3.421	3.241	3.076	2.925
9	4.303	4.163	4.031	3.905	3.786	3.673	3.566	3.366	3.184	3.019
10	4.494	4.339	4.192	4.054	3.923	3.799	3.682	3.465	3.269	3.092
11	4.656	4.486	4.327	4.177	4.035	3.902	3.776	3.543	3.335	3.147
12	4.793	4.611	4.439	4.278	4.127	3.985	3.851	3.606	3.387	3.190
13	4.910	4.715	4.533	4.362	4.203	4.053	3.912	3.656	3.427	3.223
14	5.008	4.802	4.611	4.432	4.265	4.108	3.962	3.695	3.459	3.249
15	5.092	4.876	4.675	4.489	4.315	4.153	4.001	3.726	3.483	3.268

Glossary of terms

Accounting period

The period of time between two reporting dates.

Accounting policies

These are disclosed in the annual reports published by quoted companies and represent the interpretation of accounting principles and requirements adopted by the board of directors.

Accounting practices

The practices governing the preparation of annual reports.

Accounting principles

These are often referred to as generally accepted accounting principles (GAAP). They are only generally accepted and do not have the force of law. You should note that sometimes they are referred to as accounting concepts and conventions.

Accounting rate of return

The return generated by an investment opportunity expressed as a percentage of the capital outlay.

Acquisition

The process by which a company acquires a controlling interest in the voting shares of another company.

Amortisation

The writing off of and asset over a period. It is often used in conjunction with intangible assets, e.g. goodwill.

Annual report

A set of statements usually comprising chairman's statement, report of directors, review of operation together with financial statements and notes. Principally for the shareholders, although many other interested parties.

Annuity

Is a series of payments of an equal, or constant, amount of money at fixed intervals for a specified number of periods.

Arbitrage Pricing Theory (APT)

The principle which underpins APT is that two assets that have identical risk characteristics must offer the same return or an arbitrage opportunity will exist. APT attempts to measure the various dimensions of market related risk in terms of several underlying economic factors, such as inflation, monthly production and interest rates, which systematically affect the price of all shares.

Architecture (distinctive capabilities)

Represents a unique structure of relational contracts within, or around the firm. Firms may establish these relationships with and among their employees (internal architecture), with their suppliers or customers (external architecture), or among a group of firms engaged in related activities (networks).

Audit report

A report by an auditor in accordance with the terms of appointment. Usually contains "a true and fair view" statement.

Balance sheet

A statement showing the financial position of a company as at a specified date. Records the assets and liabilities.

Bank borrowings

Includes bank overdraft and long term bank loans.

Beta

A relative measure of volatility. Relative volatility being determined by comparing a share's returns to the market's returns. The greater the volatility, the more risky the share is said to be which relates directly into a higher beta.

Business value

The value generated by the free cash flows in which *all* providers of funds have a claim.

Capital Asset Pricing Model (CAPM)

A statistical model developed in the mid-1960's, which is based upon the observation that some shares are more volatile than others. This means that when stock markets rise these shares rise faster and higher than the markets, and when the stock markets fall they fall faster and further. The return on any risky asset is the risk-free interest rate plus a risk premium which is a multiple of the beta and the premium on the market as a whole.

Capital investment appraisal

The evaluation process of proposed capital projects in fixed assets, including authorisation, implementation and control.

Capital structure

The size and composition of a company's sources of funds; equity and debt.

Cash flow "drivers"

1. Sales growth rate
2. Operating profit margin
3. Cash tax rate
4. Fixed capital investment
5. Working capital investment

Chairman's statement

A statement by the chairman of a company, normally part of the annual report, contains reference to important events.

Chaos theory

New mathematical techniques used to view the markets as complex and evolving systems.

Common-size analysis

Data in the profit and loss account and the balance sheet, expressed as a percentage of some key figure.

Compounding

A technique for determining a future value given a present value, a time period and an interest rate.

Continuing period

Time horizon beyond the planning period.

Corporate value

Where a business holds investments in other businesses the benefits of which are not captured in the business valuation process, any such benefits have to be added to determine corporate value rather than business value.

Cost of capital

Is the cost of long-term funds to a company which, to the providers of funds represents the return they will require.

Creative accounting

A number of approaches by which companies could use and have used considerable judgement to produce results which put them in the best possible light, whilst staying within the letter of the law.

Creditors

Amounts owing to trade suppliers and other sundry creditors, payable within one year.

Creditors, amounts owing within one year

Same as current liabilities.

Creditors, amounts owing after more than one year

Includes long-term loans and other liabilities.

Critical Value appraisal

Means of being able to judge whether in financial terms any benefit might result from an organisational change. The following three steps require the calculation of:

1. current market value

2. business value *as is*

3. business value with improvements.

Cross-sectional analysis

Method of estimating the cost of equity for an unquoted business entity. Cross-sectional models are also called "accounting" or "fundamental" models. They produce estimates of CAPM betas called "fundamental betas" based on underlying accounting information. A proxy for the CAPM cost of equity is then calculated using the CAPM equation.

$$K_e \quad = \quad rf \quad + \quad (Beta \ x \ Equity \ risk \ premium)$$

The bases for calculating this fundamental beta are accounting variables measuring profitability, turnover, operating characteristics, risk and size.

Current assets

Those assets in which a company trades. They include stock, debtors, short term investments, bank and cash balances.

Current liabilities

Those liabilities which a company uses to trade. They include creditors, bank overdraft, proposed final dividend, and current taxation.

Current ratio

Is the ratio of current assets divided by current liabilities. It gives an indication of a company's ability to pay its way within one year.

Current taxation

Tax payable within one year of the balance sheet date.

Debentures

A form of loan stock. Usually issued in multiples at a fixed rate of interest, repayable at a specified date.

Debtors

Amounts owed to the company by its customers.

Depreciation

An accounting adjustment to take account of the diminution in value of a fixed asset over its economic life, which affects profits by not cash flows.

Discounted cash flow

A technique reliant upon a principle which involves discounting, or scaling-down, future cash flows.

Discounting

A techniques for estimating whether a sum receivable at some time in the future is worthwhile in terms of value today.

Distinctive capabilities

- Reputation
- Architecture
- Innovation
- Strategic assets

Dividend

The proportion of the profits of a company distributed to shareholders, usually in the form of cash.

Dividend cover

A ratio showing the number of times the dividend of a company is covered out of earnings.

Dividend Valuation Model

The return shareholders will require, and hence the cost of equity to a business, can be determined with reference to the future dividend stream they require.

Dividend yield

A ratio showing the relationship between the ordinary dividend and the market price of an ordinary share.

Earnings per share

Profit attributable to shareholders before extraordinary items divided by the average number of ordinary shares in issue during the period. The calculation and result is shown by way of note in a company's annual report.

Efficient Markets Hypothesis

As far as we can tell, share prices can be trusted - given the existing stock of publicly available information shares will neither be over- nor under- valued.

Equity

The sum of issued share capital, capital reserves and revenue reserves. Is also known as shareholders interest, or net worth.

Equity risk premium

The excess return above the risk-free rate that investors demand for holding risky securities.

Equity share capital

The ordinary share capital of a company attributable to ordinary shareholders.

Financial statements

Include, profit and loss account, balance sheet and cash flow statement together with notes if applicable.

Finished goods

A term used to describe manufactured goods into store. This means that they are available for sale/despatch.

Fisher effect

The required rate of return with inflation (known as the *money* or *nominal* rate, *m*) can be calculated using the following formula:

$$(1 + m) = (1 + r)(1 + i)$$

Fixed assets

Those assets which a company needs in order to carry out trade. They consist of land and buildings, plant and machinery, vehicles, and fixtures and fittings; all at written down values.

Floating charge

See fixed charge. Given as security for debt, is a general claim against any available asset of a company.

Free cash flow

The cash available to the providers of finance.

Gearing

Expresses the relationship between some measure of interest-bearing capital and some measure of equity capital or the total capital employed.

Goodwill

The difference between the amount paid for a company as a whole and the net value of the assets and liabilities acquired.

Income statement

An American term for the profit and loss account.

Incremental Fixed Capital Investment (IFCI)

Investment in new assets to provide additional facilities to enable intended sales growth to occur.

Incremental Working Capital Investment (IWCI)

Investment in additional working capital, such as stocks of materials.

Innovation (distinctive capabilities)

A source of competitive advantage, although difficult to sustain because of the potential for replication.

Intangible assets

Those group of assets which do not physically exist, eg. goodwill, brands.

Internal rate of return (IRR)

The rate of discount which causes the total of the present value of the future cash flows to equal the initial capital outlay, i.e. at the IRR the net present value is zero.

Interest paid

The amount paid during the year on interest bearing debt.

Interim reporting

The practice adopted in the UK of issuing a brief report to shareholders on the first six months results.

Internal rate of return (IRR)

The rate of return achieved when the sum of the discounted cash flows minus the capital outlay is equal to zero (net present value is zero). Also known as the breakeven rate.

Issued share capital

The type, class and number of shares held by a company's shareholders.

Key ratio

Is a term given to the profitability ratio, in the UK this is usually defined as profit before tax plus interest paid expressed as a percentage of net capital employed.

Leverage

A USA term for gearing.

Liabilities

The financial obligations owed by a company, these can be to shareholders, other providers of debt, trade creditors and other creditors.

Liquid assets

The sum of current assets minus stock.

Liquid ratio

Is the ratio of liquid assets divided by current liabilities. It attempts to show a company's ability to pay its way in the short term.

Loan capital

Same as long-term loans.

Long-term loans

The portion of interest bearing debt which is not due for repayment within one year.

Market value of equity

The sum of market value of shares times the number of shares issued. Often referred to as market capitalisation.

MB ratio

Expresses the relationship between market value and shareholders' funds.

Minority interest

The proportion of shares in subsidiary companies which is not held by a holding company. Profit attributable to minority interests and accumulated balances are shown in the consolidated financial statements.

Net assets

The same as net capital employed.

Net capital employed

The sum of fixed assets, investments, current assets minus current liabilities.

Net current assets

Another name for net working capital.

Net present value (NPV)

A method of discounting future cash flows for an investment at a company's cost of capital then deducting the (initial) capital outlay.

Net working capital

The sum of current assets minus current liabilities.

Ordinary shares

Shares which attract the remaining profits after all other claims, and, in liquidation, the remaining assets of a company after creditors and other charges have been satisfied.

Payback period

The payback period measures how long it will take to recover the capital outlay involved in a potential investment opportunity from cash inflows.

Peer group analysis

The financial performance of a number of publicly quoted peers is used in conjunction with key financial information about the company in question.

PE ratio

One of the most significant indicators of corporate performance and it is widely quoted in the financial press. It is calculated by dividing the market price of a share by the earnings per share (or the total market value by the total profit attributable to shareholders), i.e.

$$\text{PE ratio} = \frac{\text{Market price of a share}}{\text{Earnings per share}}$$

PE Relative

$$\text{PE relative} = \frac{\text{Market price of a share}}{\text{Earnings per share}}$$

This provides a quick indication of whether a company is highly or lowly rated, although differences in the treatment of tax by individual companies do cause some distortions, such that analysts will tend to standardise their calculations.

Perpetuity

A special case of an annuity in which the cash flows are assumed to be received in perpetuity.

Planning period

The period over which competitive advantage prevails which, in simple terms we would equate with sales growth potential and the achievement of a positive net present value.

Portfolio Theory

Simply suggests that an investor who diversifies will do better than one who does not.

Present Value Rule

Why in a world of certainty accepting all projects with a positive NPV maximises the wealth of shareholders.

Price earnings ratio

Market price of an ordinary share divided by the last reported earnings per share. PE is a multiple based on the number of times earnings the market is willing to pay for a company's shares.

Profit and loss account

A statement showing the sales less the costs for the period under review. There are various "layers" of profit eg. operating profit, profit after taxation, retained profit.   Companies can adopt one of two formats for formal publication.

Quoted investments

Investments in another company which has its shares quoted on a stock exchange..

Reducing balance depreciation

A method of depreciation whereby the periodic amount written off is a percentage of the reduced balance. This results in higher charges for depreciation during the earlier life of the fixed asset with correspondingly lower charges each year.

Relevant data

Data for decision making must be *future oriented* - that is it must be *yet to be incurred*. Data about the past is irrelevant, apart from its use in forecasting.

Replacement Fixed Capital Investment (RFCI)

Investment in replacement fixed assets to maintain the level of productive facilities currently in place.

Reputation (distinctive capabilities)

Enables a company to charge premium prices, or gain larger market share at a competitive price, for a functionally equivalent product.

Reserves - capital

Is a book value which has not been generated through the normal trading activities of a company. Usually includes one-off items such as share premium, revaluation of properties.

Reserves - revenue

Is a book value which is the accumulated results of trading. Usually includes the profit and loss balance.

Residual value

Value generated beyond the planning period.

Revaluation

The periodic revaluation of fixed assets, normally land and buildings to reflect current market values. The adjustment is usually an increase in the fixed assets and a corresponding increase in the revaluation reserve.

Risk-free rate

Represents the most secure return that can be achieved.

Sales

Includes all income derived from the principal activities of a company, net of VAT.

Sensitivity analysis

Used in capital investment appraisal whereby input variables are changed to determine their effect upon a project's internal rate of return.

Share capital

Is the sum of the total number of shares issued times the nominal value of the shares.

Shareholder's funds

Another name for equity.

Shareholder value

Business value

+   Marketable securities or investments

=   Corporate value

-   Market value of debt and obligations

=   Shareholder value

Shareholder Value Analysis

Is that in broad terms the value of a business to a shareholder can be determined by discounting its future cash flows using an appropriate cost of capital.

Share premium

The difference between the price paid during the issue of share capital and the nominal value of a share. It arises due to the requirement to record issued share capital at its nominal value, therefore the balance is held in a share premium account. Share premium cannot be used to pay dividends.

Short-termism

Managing for today rather than tomorrow and beyond.

Straight line depreciation

A method of depreciation whereby an equal amount is written off a fixed asset during its estimated economic life.

Strategic assets

Sources of competitive advantage which are not based upon the distinctive capabilities of firms, but on their dominance or market position.

Strategic risk analysis

A critical step in valuation analysis and if you do not try to capture it you cannot know whether value will be created or not.

Tangible assets

An asset having a physical identity such as land and buildings, plant and machinery, vehicles etc.

Time value of money

A concept which is an integral part of the discounted cash flow technique used in capital appraisal. It recognises that cash flows in the later years of a project cannot be compared with cash flows in the earlier years.

Total assets

The sum of fixed assets plus investments plus current assets.

Total borrowings

The sum of bank borrowings, long term and short term loans.

Total debt

The sum of current liabilities plus long term loans.

Total liabilities

See total debt

Value drivers

1. Sales growth rate

2. Operating profit margin

3. Cash tax rate

4. Fixed capital investment

5. Working capital investment

6. Planning period

7. Cost of capital.

Weighted Average Cost of Capital (WACC)

A term associated with the view of there being an optimal or ideal capital structure. That is there is some mix of debt relative to equity at which the tax advantage can be maximised before the perception of debt and equity providers is of greater risk and the need to be compensated for it by demanding a higher return.

$$\text{Weighted average cost of capital} = \%\text{Debt}(K_d) + \%\text{Equity}(K_e)$$

Working capital

The excess of current assets (stock, debtors and cash) over current liabilities (creditors, bank overdraft etc).

Yield to redemption, Yield to maturity or Yield for short

The percentage which equates all future cash flows and the redemption payment with the current market value of a share.

Index

Index, Author and Company